The Selected Ninja Speedi
Cookbook for Beginners

Easy Ninja Speedi Rapid Cooker & Air Fryer Recipes Will Help

You Cook More Gourmet Food to Entertain Your Friends

Donna Vickers

CONTENTS

Introduction

The Ninja Speedi is a fantastic kitchen appliance that offers many cooking options. With its unique combination of air frying, steaming, and both functions, you can create tasty and nutritious meals that cook simultaneously on two levels. It also comes with a range of settings, including Steam & Crisp, Slow Cook, and Sous Vide, giving you even more flexibility in your cooking.

The Speedi is designed for ultimate convenience, with a lever on the lid allowing you to switch between Air Fry and Rapid Cooker modes easily. The touchscreen control panel gives you access to all 12 functions, making it super easy to operate. Whether a beginner or an experienced cook, the Ninja Speedi is simple to use and helps you cook confidently like a pro chef.

The Speedi air fryer is a must-have appliance for any kitchen. It is designed to fit easily under a cabinet with the lid down, but when used, it should be pulled out onto the countertop to provide enough space to raise the lid. This intuitive appliance has a large removable cooking pot and a crisper tray. The comprehensive manual and additional resources provide helpful tips and instructions to get you started.

For a hassle-free cooking experience, the Speedi Meal Builder offers a range of suggested food combinations and cooking times. This feature is handy if you're unsure what to cook or want to try something new. The accompanying pamphlet and booklet also provide instructions on how to make Speedi Meals, recipes, and cooking charts. Professional chefs and home cooks can benefit from the convenience and versatility of the Speedi, making it an excellent choice for anyone looking for an efficient and stress-free cooking experience.

The Ninja Speedi is an incredible kitchen gadget that provides many cooking options. Its distinctive blend of air frying, steaming, and both features allows you to whip up delicious and healthy meals that cook on two levels simultaneously. Moreover, it comes with various settings, such as Steam & Crisp, Slow Cook, and Sous Vide, providing even more versatility in your cooking.

What is Ninja Speedi ?

The Speedi air fryer is the ultimate kitchen companion for any household. It's designed to fit easily under a cabinet with the lid down, but when in use, it needs to be pulled forward on the countertop to ensure enough space to raise the lid. The Speedi has features, including a large removable cooking pot and a flat crisper tray, making it an excellent choice for cooking all sorts of dishes.

The Speedi manual and pamphlet provide clear instructions on preparing Speedi Meals and a booklet of mouth-watering recipes, colorful photos, and helpful cooking charts. Additionally, you can access the Speedi Meal Builder online, which suggests various food combinations and cooking times. With the Speedi, you can easily create professional dishes in your kitchen.

Benefits of Using It

The Speedi Meals function lets you quickly and easily make a delicious meal for up to four people in just 15 minutes.

With a 6-quart capacity, you can create a wholesome one-pot meal with your choice of base, vegetables, and protein to satisfy the whole family. The Speedi Meals function takes the guesswork out of meal planning so you can enjoy your meal quickly.

Our 12-in-1 functionality gives you maximum cooking flexibility. Rapid Cooker mode unlocks Speedi Meals, Steam

& Crisp, Steam & Bake, Steam, and Proof options. Switch to Air Fry mode and discover new culinary possibilities - including Air Fry, Bake/Roast, Broil, Dehydrate, Sear & Sauté, Slow Cook, and Sous Vide functions. With this professional-grade appliance, you'll have the power to make all your favorite dishes easily.

The Rapid Cooking System of the Speedi appliance allows you to create steam, caramelize, and air fry food simultaneously in one pot, resulting in restaurant-quality dishes. Take advantage of the Rapid Cooker mode and enjoy professional-level meals at home.

Experience the ultimate cooking convenience with SmartSwitch functionality, which allows you to easily switch between Air Fry mode and Rapid Cooker mode, opening up a world of delicious possibilities. With this professional-grade feature, you can quickly master any dish and add an extra kick of flavor to your meals. Start enjoying the convenience of SmartSwitch today and unleash your kitchen's full potential!

The Ninja Speedi Meal Builder unlocks thousands of customizable recipes tailored to the ingredients in your fridge or pantry. This easy-to-use tool helps you create the perfect dish quickly and professionally. So why wait? Start building your Speedi Meal today!

Air frying is a healthier way to prepare meals, with up to 75% less fat than traditional deep frying. We've tested it

against hand-cut, deep-fried French fries, and the results speak for themselves. Enjoy the same delicious taste without the guilt - air fry your meals today and start eating healthier! Speedi Cleanup offers a fast and easy solution to your cleanup needs. Our nonstick pot and crisper tray are dishwasher-safe, making cleaning a breeze. With this professional-grade kitchenware, you can enjoy quick and efficient cleaning in no time.

Main functions of Ninja Speedi

The Ninja Speedi is a groundbreaking appliance that offers 12 special cooking functions, providing optimal conditions for preparing delicious meals with precision.

1. SPEEDI MEALS:

This versatile appliance allows you to create two-part meals quickly with just one touch. Whether you're a seasoned chef or a home cook, you'll love how easy it is to create mouth-watering meals with the Speedi Meals function. No more guesswork in meal planning! With the Ninja Speedi, you can enjoy delicious, nutritious meals perfect for your busy lifestyle. And the best part? You won't have to compromise on taste or quality. So why wait? Try the Ninja Speedi today and savor every delectable bite!

2. STEAM & CRISP:

Experience the ultimate blend of juicy and crispy results with the perfect balance of moisture and crunch, thanks to the Steam & Crisp function. This innovative feature is designed to cater to professional chefs and home cooks, offering the convenience and ease of use needed to prepare perfectly cooked food every time. Enjoy healthier meals with reduced fat and calories while savoring your favorite dishes' satisfying texture and flavor. Trust in the Steam & Crisp function to create mouth-watering meals you feel good about.

3. STEAM & CRISP BAKE:

Experience a new level of precision and control in baking with the STEAM & CRISP BAKE Function of the Ninja Speedi. You can now bake fluffier cakes and quick bread in less time and with less fat. This professional-grade baking solution is always designed to provide perfect results, allowing you to enjoy light, fluffy cakes and bread. With the Ninja Speedi, you can now easily create healthier and delicious baked goods.

4. STEAM:

The Ninja Speedi's Steam mode is perfect for gently cooking delicate foods at a high temperature. With this professional-grade cooking feature, you can enjoy perfectly cooked dishes with minimal effort. Trust in the advanced technology of the Ninja Speedi to cook your meals precisely as you intended every time.

5. PROOF:

The Ninja Speedi is a must-have appliance for professional bakers who want to craft the perfect dough for their delicious creations. Its advanced temperature and humidity controls provide the perfect environment for the dough to rest and rise, allowing bakers to create consistent and incredible results every time. With Ninja Speedi, you can be confident in your baking and enjoy delicious, perfectly risen dough for all your baked goods.

6. Air Fry:

Enjoy your favorite fried foods guilt-free with the AIR FRY Function of the Ninja Speedi. This function lets you fry your favorite foods with minimal oil, so you can indulge without worrying about extra calories. Whether you're craving crispy French fries or perfectly fried chicken, the AIR FRY Function provides a healthier alternative to traditional deep frying. So go ahead, and indulge in your favorite fried foods while still maintaining a healthy and fit lifestyle.

7. BAKE/ROAST

Looking to quickly and easily roast meats, vegetables, and more? The Bake/Roast function on the Ninja Speedi is the perfect solution. It transforms your appliance into an efficient roaster oven that maintains the flavor and texture of your food. Whether you're cooking for a large group or meal prepping for the week, Bake/Roast is the perfect solution. With this function, you can easily enjoy delicious, perfectly cooked baked treats and tender roasted meats in no time.

8. Broil:

Add texture, color, and crispness to your meals with the Ninja Speedi's Caramelize Function. This advanced cooking method allows you to create healthy, delectable, crispy and caramelized dishes. From melting cheese on burgers and pasta to caramelizing sugar on top of pudding and Brulee, this function offers endless possibilities to experiment with different recipes and enhance the flavor of your ingredients. With this innovative technique, you can make your meals healthier and tastier, unlocking a new level of culinary creativity.

9. DEHYDRATE:

Its advanced dehydrating function lets you enjoy the best dry food without expensive dehydrators. This function simplifies your kitchen setup by eliminating the need for overpriced and complicated dehydrators, making it an ideal choice for professionals and health-conscious individuals. Get ready to experience the convenience and high-quality results of Ninja Speedi for all your dehydrated food needs.

10. SOUS VIDE:

With sous vide, you have complete control over the temperature to achieve perfect results. High-end restaurants have used this cooking method for years to ensure that each dish is cooked to the ideal level of doneness. With the Ninja Speedi, you can now bring the same precision and quality to your home cooking, enjoying restaurant-quality meals every time.

11. SLOW COOK:

The Slow Cooker Mode of the Ninja Speedi is the ultimate solution for perfectly cooked meals without spending all day in the kitchen. This innovative mode lets you cook your food at a lower temperature for extended periods, freeing up your time for other activities. With the Ninja Speedi Slow Cooker Mode, you can enjoy delicious, high-quality meals without compromising your busy schedule.

12. SEAR/SAUTÉ:

With its professional stovetop tools, the Ninja Speedi now allows you to achieve restaurant-quality cooking in your own kitchen. You can easily create gourmet-level dishes quickly and precisely with the ability to brown meats, sauté vegetables, simmer sauces, and more. Enjoy the convenience and high-quality results of a professional stovetop right at home with your Ninja Speedi.

Step-By-Step Using Ninja Speedi

SPEEDI MEALS:

1. Make sure to remove the Crisper Tray from the bottom of the pot before starting.
2. Follow the recipe instructions to add the liquid and ingredients to the pot's bottom.
3. Extend the legs on the Crisper Tray, and put the tray in the raised position inside the pot. Then, add the ingredients to the tray as specified in the recipe.
4. Switch the SmartSwitch to the RAPID COOKER setting, and use the center arrows to select Speedi Meals. The default setting will show up on display. Adjust the temperature by using the up and down arrows to the left of the display in increments of 10 or 15 degrees from 250°F to 450°F.
5. Modify the cooking time by using the arrows on the right of the display, in 1-minute steps, up to a maximum of 30 minutes.
6. Press START/STOP to start cooking.
7. The progress bars on display will indicate that the unit is generating steam. Once the steam level reaches the appropriate

level, the timer will start counting down.

8. When the cooking time runs out, the unit will beep and display "End." If your food needs additional cooking time, use the up arrows on the right of the display to increase the cooking time.

STEAM & CRISP:

1. Collect all the ingredients specified in your recipe.

2. Set the SmartSwitch to the RAPID COOKER mode, and select Steam & Crisp using the center front arrows. The default setting will appear on display.

3. Adjust the temperature by using the up and down arrows to the left of the display in increments of 10 or 15 degrees between 250°F and 450°F.

4. Modify the cooking time by using the arrows to the right of the display, in 1-minute steps, up to a maximum of 30 minutes.

5. Press START/STOP to begin cooking. The progress bars on display will show that the unit is building steam.

6. The timer will start counting down once the unit reaches the proper steam level.

7. When the cooking time reaches zero, the unit will beep and display "End." If your food needs more cooking time, use the up arrow on the right of the display to add extra time. The unit will skip the preheating process.

STEAM & BAKE:

1. Start by placing the Crisper Tray at the bottom and the baking accessories on top of your RAPID COOKER.

2. Set the SmartSwitch to the RAPID COOKER mode, and use the center arrows to select STEAM & BAKE.

3. The default temperature setting will appear on display, and you can adjust it using the up and down arrows on the left in 10 or 15-degree increments between 250°F and 400°F.

4. To adjust the cooking time, use the up and down arrows on the right of the display to set a time between 1 minute and 1 hour and 15 minutes in 1-minute steps.

5. Press START/STOP when you're ready to start cooking. The progress bars on display will indicate the unit is building steam. The timer will begin counting down once preheating is finished.

6. When the cooking time expires, the unit will beep and display "End." If you need to cook the food further, press the up arrow on the right of the display to add extra time.

7. The unit will skip the preheating step for additional cooking.

STEAM:

1. Start by adding water to the bottom of the pot, and place the Crisper Tray in the bottom position. Then add your desired ingredients.

2. Set the SmartSwitch to the RAPID COOKER mode, and use the center front arrows to select STEAM.

3. Use the up and down arrows on the right of the display to adjust the cooking time.

4. Once you've set the cooking time, press START/STOP to begin cooking.

5. The unit will preheat to bring the liquid to a boil. The progress bars on display will indicate the unit is building steam. When the preheating is finished, the timer will start counting down. The preheating animation will appear on the display until the unit reaches temperature, and then switch to the timer counting down.

6. When the cooking time is up, the unit will beep and display "End." By following these steps, you can ensure a successful cooking experience

PROOF:

1. Place the Crisper Tray at the bottom of the pot and add dough to the baking accessory. Place the accessory on top of the tray.

2. Set the SmartSwitch to the RAPID COOKER setting, and use the center front arrows to select PROOF. The default temperature setting will display. Adjust the temperature from 90°F to 105°F in 5-degree increments using the up and

down arrows to the left of the display.

3. Adjust the proof time from 15 minutes to 4 hours in 5-minute increments using the up and down arrows to the right of the display.

4. Press START/STOP to start proofing.

5. When the proofing time reaches zero, the unit will beep and display "End." Follow these steps carefully for successful proofing.

SEAR/SAUTÉ:

1. To begin cooking, remove the Crisper Tray from the pot and add your ingredients.

2. Move the SmartSwitch to AIR FRY/STOVETOP and use the center front arrows to select the desired heat setting, ranging from "Lo1" to "Hi5".

3. Press START/STOP to start cooking, and the timer will begin counting up. To stop the SEAR/SAUTÉ function, press START/STOP. If you want to switch to a different cooking function, first press START/STOP to end the current function, and then use the SmartSwitch and center front arrows to choose your desired function.

SLOW COOK:

1. Remove the crisper tray before adding your ingredients to the slow cooker pot. Check the maximum fill line (indicated inside the pot) to avoid overfilling.

2. Move the SmartSwitch to AIR FRY/STOVETOP and select SLOW COOK using the center front arrows. The default temperature setting will appear on display. Use the up and down arrows to the left of the display to choose between "Hi," "Lo," or "BUFFET" settings.

3. Use the up and down arrows to the right of the display to adjust the cooking time. Press START/STOP to begin the cooking process.

4. When the cooking time is up, the unit will beep and automatically switch to Keep Warm mode while counting up.

SOUS VIDE:

1. Before starting the sous vide process, remove the crisper

tray from the pot and add 12 cups of room-temperature water to the marked level.

2. Close the lid and select AIR FRY/STOVETOP on the dial, then use the center arrows to choose SOUS VIDE. The default temperature setting will be displayed. Use the up and down arrows to the left of the display to set a temperature in 5-degree increments from 120°F to 190°F.

3. The default cook time is 3 hours, but you can adjust the time in 15-minute increments up to 12 hours, then in 1-hour increments up to 24 hours, using the up and down arrows on the right of the display.

4. Press START/STOP to begin preheating. The unit will beep when preheating is complete, and the display will show "ADD FOOD." To place the bags in the water, use the water displacement method: Leave a corner of the bag unzipped and slowly lower the bag into the water, allowing the water pressure to force the air out of the bag and causing it to submerge. Repeat for each bag.

Air Fry:

1. Prepare your cooking station by placing your Crisper Tray in the bottom position.

2. Next, add your desired ingredients to the pot and close the lid. Switch the SmartSwitch to AIR FRY/STOVETOP, and the unit will default to AIR FRY mode.

3. The default temperature will be displayed, but for precise cooking, use the up and down arrows on the left side of the display to choose a temperature between 250°F and 400°F in 10 or 15-degree increments.

4. Adjust the cooking time as needed using the up and down arrows on the right side of the display, with increments of 1 minute up to 1 hour.

5. Press START/STOP to begin cooking and let the unit work its magic.

6. When the cooking time reaches zero, the unit will beep and display "End," indicating that your meal is ready. Follow these professional and easy-to-follow instructions

for delicious results every time!

BAKE/ROAST

1. Before starting the cooking process, ensure that the Crisper Tray is placed at the bottom of the pot.

2. Move the SmartSwitch to AIR FRY/STOVETOP, and then use the center front arrows to select the BAKE/ROAST option.

3. The default temperature setting will be displayed. To achieve precise cooking, use the up and down arrows to the left of the display to choose a temperature between 300°F to 400°F with increments of either 10 or 15 degrees.

4. The up and down arrows to the right of the display can be used to set the cooking time up to 1 hour in 1-minute increments or from 1 hour to 4 hours in 5-minute increments.

5. Finally, press START/STOP to begin the cooking process. When the cooking time reaches zero, the unit will beep, and the display will show "End."

6. With these simple steps, you can achieve the perfect bake or roast every time.

Broil:

1. Place the ingredients on the Crisper Tray in an elevated position before closing the lid for optimal results.

2. Then, move the SmartSwitch to AIR FRY/STOVETOP

and select BROIL using the center front arrows. The default temperature setting will be displayed, and you can set the temperature between 400°F to 450°F in 25-degree increments using the up and down arrows to the left of the display.

3. You can adjust the cooking time to 30 minutes in 1-minute increments using the up and down arrows to the right of the display. Press START/STOP to begin cooking.

4. The unit will beep and display "End" when the cooking time reaches zero. Follow these simple steps for perfectly broiled dishes every time.

DEHYDRATE:

1. Before starting your dehydrating session, place the Crisper Tray at the bottom of the pot.

2. Move the SmartSwitch to AIR FRY/STOVETOP and select DEHYDRATE with the center front arrows. The default temperature setting will be displayed. You can adjust the temperature between 105°F and 195°F by using the up and down arrows to the left of the display.

3. To adjust the cooking time, use the up and down arrows to the right of the display. You can set the cooking time between 1 and 12 hours in 15-minute increments.

4. Press START/STOP to begin the dehydrating process.

5. When the cooking time reaches zero, the unit will beep,

and the display will show "End" to indicate the end of the cooking session. Follow these steps for successful and efficient dehydration.

Tips for Using Accessories

Remove and dispose of all packaging materials, stickers, and tape before using your unit.

It is crucial to carefully read and follow the operational instructions, warnings, and necessary safeguards to ensure the safety of yourself and your property.

For optimal operation, wash the removable pot, crisper tray, and condensation collector in warm, soapy water, then rinse and dry them thoroughly.

Cleaning and Caring for Ninja Speedi

To ensure that your Ninja Speedi operates optimally, cleaning it thoroughly before and after each use is essential. Here are the steps to follow for proper cleaning:

Before beginning the cleaning process, disconnect the central unit from the power source.

Use a damp cloth to wipe down the main unit and control panel.

Dishwasher-safe accessories like the basket and crisper plate can be placed in the dishwasher.

Soak plates with tough food residues in warm soapy water to remove them.

Dry all parts with a towel or allow them to air dry.

Following these steps, you can ensure your Ninja Speedi is properly cleaned and ready to provide optimal performance.

Frequently Asked Questions & Notes

1. The Steam function on the unit generates significant amounts of steam.

Steam is released through the vent during cooking is a regular occurrence.

2. An error message reading "ADD POT" is displayed on the screen.

The unit displays an "ADD POT" error message when the complete meal pot is not placed inside the cooker base, as it is required for all functions.

4-Week Meal Plan

Week 1	Week 2

Week 1

Day 1:
Breakfast: Breakfast Nutty Cinnamon Buns
Lunch: Creamy Spaghetti Squash
Snack: Chipotle Bacon-Jicama Hash
Dinner: Herbed Salmon Fillets
Dessert: Easy Cardamom Custard

Day 2:
Breakfast: Mini Beef Cheeseburger Sliders
Lunch: Parmesan Broccoli
Snack: Sautéed Spinach with Bacon & Shallots
Dinner: Mini Meat Loaves
Dessert: Yummy Mixed Berry Crumble

Day 3:
Breakfast: Spinach Quiche
Lunch: Honey Glazed Carrots
Snack: Homemade Bacon-Wrapped Sausage Skewers
Dinner: Spicy Chicken Cutlets
Dessert: Sweet Pineapple Spears

Day 4:
Breakfast: Crispy Chicken Tenders
Lunch: Breaded Buffalo Cauliflower
Snack: Air Fried Brussels Sprouts & Bacon
Dinner: Juicy Pork Loin Roast
Dessert: Maple Bread Pudding

Day 5:
Breakfast: Breakfast Tomato & Sausage Frittata
Lunch: Air Fried Sweet Potatoes
Snack: Cheese Ham Rolls
Dinner: Simple Air-Fried Shrimp
Dessert: Chocolate Brownies

Day 6:
Breakfast: Sausage and Tomato Egg Toast
Lunch: Rosemary Sweet Potato Bites
Snack: Cheesy Broccoli
Dinner: Lime Hot Chicken Wings
Dessert: Glazed Rainbow Donuts

Day 7:
Breakfast: Peanut Butter & Banana Sandwich
Lunch: Teriyaki Tofu "Steaks"
Snack: Garlicky Parmesan Cauliflower
Dinner: Pepperoni Bread Pockets
Dessert: Gluten-Free Chocolate Donut Holes

Week 2

Day 1:
Breakfast: Breakfast Zucchini Muffins
Lunch: Mexican Street Corn Kernels
Snack: Lemony Sugar Snap Peas
Dinner: Cheese Chicken Quesadilla
Dessert: Lemony Apple Turnovers

Day 2:
Breakfast: Cheese & Egg Sandwich
Lunch: Charred Green Beans
Snack: Flaxseed Cheese Chips
Dinner: Crispy Cod Sticks
Dessert: Blueberry Frosted Pies

Day 3:
Breakfast: Crispy Avocado Fries
Lunch: Classic French Fries
Snack: Lemon-Garlic Bacon & Swiss Chard
Dinner: Tasty Pizza Tortilla Rolls
Dessert: Apple Fritters

Day 4:
Breakfast: Delicious Asparagus Omelet
Lunch: Cheesy Broccoli Gratin
Snack: Herbed Cauliflower Hash
Dinner: Simple Air Fried Turkey Bacon
Dessert: Orange-Anise-Ginger Cookie

Day 5:
Breakfast: Pecans and Raisins Granola
Lunch: Garlicky Balsamic Asparagus
Snack: Homemade Mayonnaise
Dinner: Juicy Barbecued Shrimp
Dessert: Zucchini Cakes with Walnuts

Day 6:
Breakfast: Cheese Ham and Bacon Omelet
Lunch: Air Fried Corn on the Cob
Snack: Homemade Hollandaise Sauce
Dinner: Greek Lamb Pita Pockets
Dessert: Cinnamon Almonds

Day 7:
Breakfast: Salmon & Carrot Toast
Lunch: Simple Air Fried Cabbage
Snack: Buttery Green Beans and Pine Nuts
Dinner: Crispy Coconut Shrimp
Dessert: Baked Apples

Week 3

Day 1:
Breakfast: Scrambled Eggs and Bacon
Lunch: Sweet Potato Fries
Snack: Cheese-Bacon Stuffed Peppers
Dinner: Air Fried Beef Steaks
Dessert: Homemade Spice Cookies

Day 2:
Breakfast: Almond-Oats Bars
Lunch: Cheesy Hasselback Potatoes
Snack: Bacon-Wrapped Cheese Jalapeno Popper
Dinner: Coconut Chicken Tenders
Dessert: Homemade Zeppole with Cannoli Dip

Day 3:
Breakfast: Pea Protein Chicken Muffins
Lunch: Honey Cornbread
Snack: Cheesy Bacon Egg Bread
Dinner: Spicy Cod Tacos
Dessert: Lemon Ricotta Poppy Seeds Cake

Day 4:
Breakfast: Cheese Onion Omelette
Lunch: Crispy Cauliflower Nuggets
Snack: Crusted Mozzarella Sticks
Dinner: Turmeric Chicken Wings
Dessert: Coconut-Chocolate Cake

Day 5:
Breakfast: Bacon and Egg Muffins
Lunch: Sweet Acorn Squash
Snack: Bacon-Wrapped Brie Cheese
Dinner: Air Fried Pork Chops
Dessert: Chocolate Walnuts Cake

Day 6:
Breakfast: Breakfast Cheese Sandwich
Lunch: Bacon-Wrapped Asparagus
Snack: Cheese Bacon-Pepperoni Pizza
Dinner: Creamy Salmon
Dessert: Eggless Farina Cake

Day 7:
Breakfast: Blueberry and Avocado Muffins
Lunch: Cheese Tomato-Spinach Stuffed Mushrooms
Snack: Chipotle Bacon-Jicama Hash
Dinner: Air Fried Paprika Duck Skin
Dessert: Easy Cardamom Custard

Week 4

Day 1:
Breakfast: Spinach Quiche
Lunch: Kale Sushi Roll
Snack: Cheese Ham Rolls
Dinner: Air-Fried Crab Croquettes
Dessert: Sweet Pineapple Spears

Day 2:
Breakfast: Breakfast Zucchini Muffins
Lunch: Parmesan Broccoli
Snack: Cheesy Broccoli
Dinner: Lemon-Rosemary Lamb Chops
Dessert: Chocolate Brownies

Day 3:
Breakfast: Crispy Avocado Fries
Lunch: Simple Air Fried Cabbage
Snack: Garlicky Parmesan Cauliflower
Dinner: Spicy Chicken Wings
Dessert: Glazed Rainbow Donuts

Day 4:
Breakfast: Pecans and Raisins Granola
Lunch: Air Fried Sweet Potatoes
Snack: Lemony Sugar Snap Peas
Dinner: Fried Baby Squid
Dessert: Lemony Apple Turnovers

Day 5:
Breakfast: Salmon & Carrot Toast
Lunch: Honey Cornbread
Snack: Flaxseed Cheese Chips
Dinner: Delicious Beef Pies
Dessert: Apple Fritters

Day 6:
Breakfast: Almond-Oats Bars
Lunch: Crispy Cauliflower Nuggets
Snack: Herbed Cauliflower Hash
Dinner: Celery Chicken Thighs
Dessert: Orange-Anise-Ginger Cookie

Day 7:
Breakfast: Crispy Chicken Tenders
Lunch: Charred Green Beans
Snack: Cheese-Bacon Stuffed Peppers
Dinner: Crispy Calf's Liver
Dessert: Cinnamon Almonds

Blueberry and Avocado Muffins

Prep time: 10 minutes | Cook time: 10 minutes | Serves: 12

Ingredients:

2 eggs

1 cup blueberries

2 cups almond flour

1 teaspoon baking soda

⅛ teaspoon salt

2 ripe avocados, peeled, pitted, mashed

2 tablespoons liquid Stevia

1 cup plain Greek yogurt

1 teaspoon vanilla extract

For Streusel Topping:

2 tablespoons Truvia sweetener

4 tablespoons butter, softened

4 tablespoons almond flour

Directions:

1. Create the streusel topping by combining Truvia, flour, and butter until it becomes crumbly. 2. Freeze this mixture for a period of time. 3. Meanwhile, prepare the muffins by sifting flour, baking soda, baking powder, and salt together, then setting it aside. 4. In a separate bowl, mix avocados and liquid Stevia together, then add one egg at a time, beating continuously. Add vanilla extract and yogurt and continue to beat. Gradually add in the flour mixture and stir well, then gently fold in blueberries. 5. Pour the batter into greased muffin cups, filling them halfway, then sprinkle the streusel topping mixture on top. 6. Place the crisper tray in the bottom position of the pot and place muffin cups on the crisper tray. 7. Close the lid and move SmartSwitch to AIRFRY/STOVETOP. Select BAKE/ROAST, set temperature to 355°F, and set time to 10 minutes. Press START/STOP to begin cooking. 8. Once Done, remove the muffin cups from the air fryer and allow them to cool. Cool completely then serve.

Per Serving: Calories 153; Fat 11.48g; Sodium 191mg; Carbs 10.68g; Fiber 2.7g; Sugar 7.28g; Protein 3.23g

Bacon and Egg Muffins

Prep time: 8 minutes | Cook time: 6 minutes | Serves: 2

Ingredients:

2 whole wheat English muffins

4 slices of bacon

Pepper to taste

2 eggs

Directions:

1. Crack an egg each into ramekins. Season with pepper. Place the crisper tray in the bottom position of the pot, place the ramekins on the tray with the bacon alongside. 2. Close the lid and move SmartSwitch to AIRFRY/STOVETOP. Select AIR FRY, set temperature to 390°F, and set time to 6 minutes (unit will need to preheat for 5 minutes, so set an external timer if desired). Press START/STOP to begin cooking. 3. Remove the muffins from air fryer after a few minutes and split them. 4. Once the bacon and eggs are cooked, place two bacon pieces and one egg onto each egg muffin and serve right away.

Per Serving: Calories 490; Fat 32.18g; Sodium 588mg; Carbs 30.26g; Fiber 4.8g; Sugar 7.58g; Protein 21.75g

Cheese Onion Omelette

Prep time: 10 minutes | Cook time: 13 minutes | Serves: 2

Ingredients:

3 eggs

1 large yellow onion, diced

2 tablespoons cheddar cheese, shredded

½ teaspoon soy sauce

Salt and pepper to taste

Olive oil cooking spray

Directions:

1. Mix together eggs, soy sauce, pepper, and salt in a bowl. Spray with olive oil cooking spray a small pan that will fit inside of your Ninja Speedi Rapid Cooker & Air Fryer. 2. Add onions to the pan and spread them around. Place the pan on the crisper tray, then place the crisper tray in the bottom of the pot. 3. Close the lid and move SmartSwitch to AIRFRY/STOVETOP. Select AIR FRY, set temperature to 350°F, and set time to 7 minutes (unit will need to preheat for 5 minutes, so set an external timer if desired). Press START/STOP to begin cooking. 4. Pour the beaten egg mixture over the cooked onions and sprinkle the top with shredded cheese. Place back into the air fryer and cook for 6-minutes more. 5. Take out the omelet from the air fryer and serve it with toasted multi-grain bread.

Per Serving: Calories 299; Fat 20.01g; Sodium 275mg; Carbs 11.22g; Fiber 1.6g; Sugar 5.6g; Protein 18.43g

Pea Protein Chicken Muffins

Prep time: 10 minutes | Cook time: 15 minutes | Serves: 4

Ingredients:

1 cup almond flour

1 teaspoon baking powder

3 eggs

1 cup mozzarella cheese, shredded

½ cup chicken strips

3 tablespoons pea protein

1 cup cream cheese

1 cup almond milk

Directions:

1. In a mixing bowl, combine together all the ingredients and stir with wooden spoon. Fill muffin cups with the mixture ¾ full. 2. Place the muffin cups on the crisper tray, then place the crisper tray in the bottom of the pot. 3. Close the lid and move SmartSwitch to AIRFRY/STOVETOP. Select BAKE/ROAST, set temperature to 360°F, and set time to 15 minutes (unit will need to preheat for 5 minutes, so set an external timer if desired). Press START/STOP to begin cooking. 4. Enjoy!

Per Serving: Calories 488; Fat 29.76g; Sodium 665mg; Carbs 7.61g; Fiber 0.6g; Sugar 6.2g; Protein 46.24g

Almond-Oats Bars

Prep time: 10 minutes | Cook time: 17 minutes | Serves: 8

Ingredients:

2 cups old-fashioned oats

½ cup quinoa, cooked

½ cup chia seeds

½ cup prunes, pureed

¼ teaspoon salt

2 teaspoons liquid Stevia

¾ cup almond butter

½ cup dried cherries, chopped

½ cup almonds, sliced

Directions:

1. Close the lid and move SmartSwitch to AIRFRY/STOVETOP. Select AIR FRY. set temperature to 350°F, and set time to 5 minutes. Press START/STOP to begin preheating. 2. In a large mixing bowl, combine the quinoa, oats, chia seeds, cherries, almonds and stir well to mix. 3. In a saucepan over medium heat melt almond butter, liquid Stevia and coconut oil for 2-minutes and stir in the oats mixture to combine. 4. Add salt and prunes and mix well. Pour into baking dish that will fit inside of your air fryer. Place on the crisper tray, then place the crisper tray in the bottom of the pot. 5. Close the lid and cook for 15-minutes. Allow to cool for an hour once cook time is completed, then slice the bars and serve.

Per Serving: Calories 284; Fat 16g; Sodium 129mg; Carbs 36.29g; Fiber 7.6g; Sugar 2.97g; Protein 11.23g

Scrambled Eggs and Bacon

Prep time: 10 minutes | Cook time: 10 minutes | Serves: 4

Ingredients:

¼ teaspoon onion powder

4 eggs, beaten

3-ounces bacon, cooked, chopped

½ cup cheddar cheese, grated

3 tablespoons Greek yogurt

¼ teaspoon garlic powder

Salt and pepper to taste

Directions:

1. Close the lid and move SmartSwitch to AIRFRY/STOVETOP. Select BAKE/ROAST, set temperature to 330°F, and set time to 5 minutes. Press START/STOP to begin preheating. 2. In a bowl, whisk the eggs add salt and pepper to taste. Then stir in the yogurt, onion powder, garlic powder, cheese, and bacon. Add the egg mixture into a baking dish that can fit the inside of the pot. 3. Place the baking dish on the crisper tray, then place the crisper tray in the bottom of the pot. Bake for 10 minutes. Scramble eggs and serve warm.

Per Serving: Calories 275; Fat 21.9g; Sodium 526mg; Carbs 4.44g; Fiber 0.8g; Sugar 1.82g; Protein 15.88g

Salmon & Carrot Toast

Prep time: 10 minutes | Cook time: 5 minutes | Serves: 4

Ingredients:

1 lb. salmon, chopped

2 cups feta, crumbled

4 bread slices

3 tablespoons pickled red onion

2 cucumbers, sliced

1 carrot, shredded

Directions:

1. Close the lid and move SmartSwitch to AIRFRY/STOVETOP. Select AIR FRY. set temperature to 300°F, and set time to 5 minutes. Press START/STOP to begin preheating. 2. In a bowl, add salmon, feta, carrot, red onion and cucumber and mix well. 3. In a pan that can fit the inside of the pot, make a layer of bread and then pour the salmon mixture over it, you can cook in batches. 4. Place the pan on the crisper tray, then place the crisper tray in the bottom of the pot. Cook for 5 minutes.

Per Serving: Calories 434; Fat 24.81g; Sodium mg; Carbs 15.19g; Fiber 1.1g; Sugar 5.29g; Protein 36.07g

Cheese Ham and Bacon Omelet

Prep time: 10 minutes | Cook time: 10 minutes | Serves: 4

Ingredients:

4 eggs

⅓ cup ham, cooked and chopped into small pieces

⅓ cup bacon, cooked, chopped into small pieces

⅓ cup cheddar cheese, shredded

Directions:

1. Close the lid and move SmartSwitch to AIRFRY/STOVETOP. Select BAKE/ROAST, set temperature to 350°F, and set time to 5 minutes. Press START/STOP to begin preheating. 2. Combine the eggs, add the ham, bacon, and cheese in a medium bowl and stir well. Add the mixture to a baking pan that is sprayed with cooking spray. 3. Place the pan on the crisper tray, then place the crisper tray in the bottom of the pot. Cook for 10 minutes. 4. When cooking time is completed, serve warm.

Per Serving: Calories 220; Fat 16.85g; Sodium 478mg; Carbs 2g; Fiber 0.3g; Sugar 0.79g; Protein 14.87g

Pecans and Raisins Granola

Prep time: 10 minutes | Cook time: 5 minutes | Serves: 6

Ingredients:

1½ cups rolled oats

½ cup pecans, roughly chopped

Dash of salt

½ cup raisins

½ cup sunflower seeds

2 tablespoons butter, melted

2 teaspoons liquid Stevia

Directions:

1. Close the lid and move SmartSwitch to AIRFRY/STOVETOP. Select BAKE/ROAST, set temperature to 350°F, and set time to 5 minutes. Press START/STOP to begin preheating. 2. Add oats, pecans and a dash of salt to a mixing bowl and stir well. In a separate small bowl, mix butter with Stevia, then add to oat mixture. 3. Spray the inside of a baking pan with cooking spray and add in the oat mixture. Place on the crisper tray, then place the crisper tray in the bottom of the pot. Cook for 5 minutes. Stir halfway through the cooking time. 4. Remove from the rack and pour into a bowl to cool. 5. Add the sunflower seeds and raisins and stir. Eat immediately or store in airtight container.

Per Serving: Calories 218; Fat 17.49g; Sodium 58mg; Carbs 19.13g; Fiber 5.4g; Sugar 1.01g; Protein 7.32g

Delicious Asparagus Omelet

Prep time: 10 minutes | Cook time: 8 minutes | Serves: 2

Ingredients:

3 eggs

5 steamed asparagus tips

2 tablespoons of warm milk

1 tablespoon parmesan cheese, grated

Salt and pepper to taste

Non-stick cooking spray

Directions:

1. Close the lid and move SmartSwitch to AIRFRY/STOVETOP. Select BAKE/ROAST, set temperature to 320°F, and set time to 5 minutes. Press START/STOP to begin preheating. 2. In a large bowl, combine the eggs, milk, cheese, salt and pepper then blend them. 3. Spray a baking pan with non-stick cooking spray. Pour the egg mixture into pan and add the asparagus then place pan on the crisper tray, then place the crisper tray in the bottom of the pot. 4. Bake for 8-minutes. Serve warm.

Per Serving: Calories 226; Fat 15.82g; Sodium 207mg; Carbs 5.09g; Fiber 0.5g; Sugar 3.05g; Protein 15.28g

Crispy Avocado Fries

Prep time: 10 minutes | Cook time: 8 minutes | Serves: 2

Ingredients:

2 eggs, beaten

2 large avocados, peeled, pitted, cut into 8 slices each

¼ teaspoon pepper

½ teaspoon cayenne pepper

Salt to taste

Juice of ½ a lemon

½ cup of whole wheat flour

1 cup whole wheat breadcrumbs

Greek yogurt to serve

Directions:

1. Close the lid and move SmartSwitch to AIRFRY/STOVETOP. Select AIR FRY. set temperature to 390°F, and set time to 5 minutes. Press START/STOP to begin preheating. 2. In a bowl, mix together the flour, salt, pepper and cayenne pepper. Add bread crumbs into another bowl. Beat eggs in a third bowl. 3. Coat the avocado slices in the flour mixture, dip them in the egg mixture, and then cover them in breadcrumbs. 4. Place avocado fries on the crisper tray, then place the crisper tray in the bottom of the pot. Air fry for 6minutes. 5. When cook time is complete, transfer the avocado fries onto a serving platter. 6. Sprinkle with lemon juice and serve with Greek yogurt.

Per Serving: Calories 763; Fat 41.47g; Sodium 274mg; Carbs 84.55g; Fiber 23.3g; Sugar 2.98g; Protein 25.09g

Cheese & Egg Sandwich

Prep time: 10 minutes | Cook time: 6 minutes | Serves: 1

Ingredients:

1-2 eggs

1-2 slices of cheddar or Swiss cheese

A bit of butter

1 roll sliced in half (your choice), Kaiser bun, English muffin, etc.

Directions:

1. Close the lid and move SmartSwitch to AIRFRY/STOVETOP. Select AIR FRY. set temperature to 390°F, and set time to 5 minutes. Press START/STOP to begin preheating. 2. Butter your sliced roll on both sides. Place the eggs in an oven-safe dish and whisk. Add seasoning if you wish such as dill, chives, oregano, and salt. 3. Place the egg dish, roll and cheese on the crisper tray, then place the crisper tray in the bottom of the pot. Cook for 6 minutes. 4. After the air fryer has finished cooking, take out the ingredients. 5. Then, put the egg and cheese in between the pieces of roll and serve it warm. 6. If you want, you can consider adding slices of avocado and tomatoes to this breakfast sandwich!

Per Serving: Calories 517; Fat 34.05g; Sodium 634mg; Carbs 23.48g; Fiber 0.9g; Sugar 3.77g; Protein 27.82g

Breakfast Zucchini Muffins

Prep time: 10 minutes | Cook time: 12 minutes | Serves: 5

Ingredients:

1 tablespoon cream cheese

Half a cup zucchini, shredded

1 tablespoon plain yogurt

1 egg

1 cup of milk

2 tablespoons of warmed coconut oil

Pinch of sea salt

2 teaspoons baking powder

1 teaspoon cinnamon

1 tablespoon liquid Stevia

4 cups whole wheat flour

Directions:

1. Close the lid and move SmartSwitch to AIRFRY/STOVETOP. Select AIR FRY. set temperature to 350°F, and set time to 5 minutes. Press START/STOP to begin preheating. 2. Combine flour, sea salt, baking powder, and cinnamon in a mixing bowl. 3. In another bowl, mix together coconut oil, milk, yogurt, liquid Stevia, and egg until well blended. 4. Then, combine the dry and wet ingredients in a large bowl and use a hand mixer to blend them. Add shredded zucchini to the mixture and fold in the cream cheese. 5. Place five muffin cups on the crisper tray, then place the crisper tray in the bottom of the pot. Fill each cup ¾ full of mixture. Cook for 12 minutes. Serve warm or cold.

Per Serving: Calories 448; Fat 12.5g; Sodium 178mg; Carbs 74.2g; Fiber 10.8g; Sugar 3.81g; Protein 16.68g

Peanut Butter & Banana Sandwich

Prep time: 10 minutes | Cook time: 6 minutes | Serves: 1

Ingredients:

2 slices of whole wheat bread

1 teaspoon of sugar-free maple syrup

1 sliced banana

2 tablespoons of peanut butter

Directions:

1. Close the lid and move SmartSwitch to AIRFRY/STOVETOP. Select AIR FRY. set temperature to 330°F, and set time to 5 minutes. Press START/STOP to begin preheating. 2. Spread peanut butter evenly on both sides of the bread slices. 3. Place the sliced banana on top and then drizzle with sugar-free maple syrup. 4. Place on the crisper tray, then place the crisper tray in the bottom of the pot. Cook for 6 minutes. 5. Serve warm.

Per Serving: Calories 456; Fat 11.24g; Sodium 821mg; Carbs 82.99g; Fiber 9.4g; Sugar 24.13g; Protein 11.45g

Sausage and Tomato Egg Toast

Prep time: 10 minutes | Cook time: 10 minutes | Serves: 2

Ingredients:

⅛ teaspoon of black pepper

¼ teaspoon salt

½ teaspoon Italian seasoning

¼ teaspoon balsamic vinegar

¼ teaspoon sugar-free maple syrup

1 cup sausages, chopped into small pieces

2 eggs

2 slices of whole wheat toast

3 tablespoons cheddar cheese, shredded

6-slices tomatoes

Cooking spray

A little mayonnaise to serve

Directions:

1. Close the lid and move SmartSwitch to AIRFRY/STOVETOP. Select AIR FRY. set temperature to 320°F, and set time to 5 minutes. Press START/STOP to begin preheating. 2. S pray a baking dish that can fit your pot with cooking spray. Place the bread slices at the bottom of dish. 3. Then sprinkle sausages on top of the bread, followed by laying tomatoes over them. Sprinkle some cheese on the top. 4. Beat the eggs and pour them over the bread slices. Drizzle some vinegar and maple syrup over the eggs. 5. Add Italian seasoning, salt, and pepper to taste. Finish it off by sprinkling more cheese on top. 6. Place the baking dish on the crisper tray, then place the crisper tray in the bottom of the pot. Cook for 10 minutes. 7. Remove from air fryer and add spot of mayonnaise and serve.

Per Serving: Calories 358; Fat 22.21g; Sodium 904mg; Carbs 17.39g; Fiber 3.1g; Sugar 3.74g; Protein 21.63g

Breakfast Cheese Sandwich

Prep time: 10 minutes | Cook time: 5 minutes | Serves: 2

Ingredients:

4 slices of brown bread

½ cup sharp cheddar cheese, shredded

¼ cup butter, melted

Directions:

1. Put cheese and butter in different bowls. 2. Melt the butter and apply it to all 4 slices of bread using a brush. 3. Then, place the cheese on 2 of the slices of bread. Put sandwiches together and place them on the crisper tray, then place the crisper tray in the bottom of the pot. 4. Close the lid and move SmartSwitch to AIRFRY/STOVETOP. Select AIR FRY. Cook at 360°F for 5 minutes and serve warm.

Per Serving: Calories 494; Fat 33.94g; Sodium 932mg; Carbs 39.36g; Fiber 4.42g; Sugar 2.27g; Protein 11.71g

Breakfast Tomato & Sausage Frittata

Prep time: 10 minutes | Cook time: 10 minutes | Serves: 3

Ingredients:

6 eggs

8 cherry tomatoes, halved

2 tablespoons parmesan cheese, shredded

1 Italian sausage, diced

Salt and pepper to taste

Directions:

1. Close the lid and move SmartSwitch to AIRFRY/STOVETOP. Select BAKE/ROAST, set temperature to 335°F, and set time to 5 minutes. Press START/STOP to begin preheating. 2. Add the tomatoes and sausage to a baking dish that can fit your pot. 3. Place the baking dish on the crisper tray, then place the crisper tray in the bottom of the pot. Cook for 5 minutes. 4. In the meantime, put eggs, cheese, salt, pepper, and oil in a mixing bowl and stir thoroughly. 5. Remove the baking dish from the pot and pour the egg mixture on top, spreading evenly. 6. Placing the dish back into the pot and bake for an additional 5 minutes. 7. Remove from the pot and slice into wedges and serve.

Per Serving: Calories 343; Fat 22.48g; Sodium 405mg; Carbs 13.16g; Fiber 2.4g; Sugar 2.07g; Protein 23.5g

Crispy Chicken Tenders

Prep time: 10 minutes | Cook time: 10 minutes | Serves: 4

Ingredients:

¾ lb. of chicken tenders

For Breading:

2 tablespoons olive oil

1 teaspoon black pepper

½ teaspoon salt

½ cup seasoned breadcrumbs

½ cup all-purpose flour

2 eggs, beaten

Directions:

1. Close the lid and move SmartSwitch to AIRFRY/STOVETOP. Select AIR FRY. set temperature to 330°F, and set time to 5 minutes. Press START/STOP to begin preheating. 2. Prepare three bowls by placing breadcrumbs, eggs, and flour in each of them. 3. Season the breadcrumbs with salt and pepper, and then add olive oil and mix well. 4. Take the chicken tenders and dip them first in the flour, then in the eggs, and finally in the breadcrumbs. 5. Press the chicken gently to make sure that the breadcrumbs evenly coat the chicken. Shake off any excess. 6. Place the coated chicken on the crisper tray, then place the crisper tray in the bottom of the pot. 7. Cook the chicken tenders for 10 minutes in the air fryer. Serve warm.

Per Serving: Calories 409; Fat 22.85g; Sodium 743mg; Carbs 29.99g; Fiber 0.7g; Sugar 0.62g; Protein 20.47g

Spinach Quiche

Ingredients:

2 eggs

1 large yellow onion, diced

1¾ cups whole wheat flour

1½ cups spinach, chopped

¾ cup cottage cheese

Salt and black pepper to taste

2 tablespoons olive oil

¼ cup butter

¼ cup milk

Directions:

1. In a bowl, mix together the flour, salt, butter, and milk, knead dough until smooth and refrigerate for 15-minutes. Remove the crisper tray from the pot. Add the oil to the pot. 2. Move the SmartSwitch to AIRFRY/ STOVETOP. Select SEAR/ SAUTÉ, set temperature to 3. 3. When the oil is hot, add the onions into the pot and sauté them. Add spinach and cook until it wilts. 4. Drain excess moisture from spinach. Press START/STOP to end the cooking function. 5. Transfer the spinach mixture to a plate, set aside. Beat the eggs and mix in cheese in a bowl. Retrieve the dough from the refrigerator and divide it into 8 equal portions. 6. Form each portion into a round shape that fits the quiche mold's base. Put the rolled dough into the molds, and add the spinach filling on top of the dough. 7. Then, place the dough on the crisper tray, then place the crisper tray in the bottom of the pot. Select AIR FRY function, set temperature to 355°F, and set time to 15 minutes. Press START/STOP to begin cooking. 8. When cooking is complete, serve warm or cold.

Per Serving: Calories 949; Fat 53.39g; Sodium 609mg; Carbs 90.67g; Fiber 13.3g; Sugar 9.16g; Protein 34.72g

Mini Beef Cheeseburger Sliders

Ingredients:

1 lb. ground beef

6 slices of cheddar cheese

6 dinner rolls

Salt and black pepper to taste

Directions:

1. Close the lid and move SmartSwitch to AIRFRY/STOVETOP. Select AIR FRY. set temperature to 390°F, and set time to 5 minutes. Press START/STOP to begin preheating. 2. Form 6 beef patties each about 2.5 ounces and season with salt and black pepper. Place the burger patties on the crisper tray, then place the crisper tray in the bottom of the pot. Cook them for 10 minutes. 3. Remove the burger patties from the air fryer; place the cheese over the burgers, then put them back in the air fryer to cook for one more minute. 4. After that, take the burgers out and put them on dinner rolls. Serve while they're still warm.

Per Serving: Calories 355; Fat 19.64g; Sodium 374mg; Carbs 13.96g; Fiber 1.2g; Sugar 0.92g; Protein 29.41g

Breakfast Nutty Cinnamon Buns

Prep time: 10 minutes | Cook time: 30 minutes | Serves: 9

Ingredients:

¾ cup unsweetened almond milk

4 tablespoons sugar-free maple syrup

½ cup pecan nuts, toasted

3 teaspoons cinnamon powder

1½ cups almond flour, sifted

1 cup whole grain flour, sifted

1 tablespoon coconut oil, melted

3 tablespoons water

1 tablespoon ground flaxseed

1½ tablespoons active yeast

2 ripe bananas, sliced

4 dates, pitted

¼ cup icing sugar

Directions:

1. First, warm up the almond milk and mix in the syrup and yeast. Let the yeast sit for 10 minutes to activate. 2. In a separate bowl, mix the flaxseed and water to make an egg substitute and let it soak for 2 minutes. Add coconut oil and combine it with the yeast mixture. 3. In a different bowl, mix both types of flour and 2 teaspoons of cinnamon powder. 4. Pour this mixture into the yeast-flaxseed mixture and combine it until a dough is formed. Knead the dough on a floured surface for about 10 minutes. 5. Place the kneaded dough into a greased bowl and cover it with a tea towel. Leave it in a warm and dark area to rise for 1 hour. 6. To make the filling, mix the pecans, dates, and banana slices with the remaining teaspoon of cinnamon powder. 7. Close the lid and move SmartSwitch to AIRFRY/STOVETOP. Select AIR FRY. set temperature to 390°F, and set time to 5 minutes. Press START/STOP to begin preheating. 8. Roll the risen dough on a floured surface until it is thin. Spread the pecan mixture over the dough. Roll dough and cut it into nine slices. 9. Place inside of a dish that will fit into the pot. Place the dish on the crisper tray, then place the crisper tray in the bottom of the pot. Cook for 30-minutes. 10. Once cooking time is completed, sprinkle with icing sugar.

Per Serving: Calories 161; Fat 7.17g; Sodium 45mg; Carbs 24.13g; Fiber 4.5g; Sugar 7.41g; Protein 4.14g

Chapter 2 Vegetable and Sides Recipes

Creamy Spaghetti Squash

Prep time: 10 minutes | Cook time: 30 minutes | Serves: 2

Ingredients:

spaghetti squash

1 tsp. olive oil

Salt and pepper

4 tbsp. heavy cream

1 tsp. butter

Directions:

1. Close the lid and move SmartSwitch to AIRFRY/STOVETOP. Select AIR FRY. set temperature to 360°F, and set time to 5 minutes. Press START/STOP to begin preheating. 2. Cut and de-seed the spaghetti squash. Brush with the olive oil and season with salt and pepper to taste. 3. Put the squash on the crisper tray, with the cut-side-down. Then place the tray in the bottom of the pot. Cook for 30 minutes. 4. While cooking the spaghetti inside the squash, use a fork to separate and stir it halfway through. 5. After the squash is fully cooked, continue to separate the spaghetti with the fork and mix it with heavy cream and butter. 6. Finally, serve it with your preferred low-carb tomato sauce.

Per Serving: Calories 213; Fat 15.47g; Sodium 119mg; Carbs 19.43g; Fiber 3.2g; Sugar 5.52g; Protein 2.37g

Garlicky Balsamic Asparagus

Prep time: 10 minutes | Cook time: 10 minutes | Serves: 4

Ingredients:

1-pound asparagus

2 tablespoons olive oil

1 tablespoon balsamic vinegar

2 teaspoons minced garlic

Salt

Freshly ground black pepper

Directions:

1. Remove the white end of the asparagus by cutting or snapping it off. Then, mix the asparagus with olive oil, garlic, vinegar, salt, and pepper in a big bowl. 2. Close the lid and move SmartSwitch to AIRFRY/STOVETOP. Select AIR FRY. set temperature to 400°F, and set time to 5 minutes. Press START/STOP to begin preheating. 3. Using your hands, gently mix all the ingredients together, making sure that the asparagus is thoroughly coated. 4. Lay out the asparagus on the crisper tray, then place the crisper tray in the bottom of the pot. Cook for 10 minutes. 5. Using tongs, flip the asparagus halfway through the cooking time.

Per Serving: Calories 88; Fat 6.9g; Sodium 149mg; Carbs 5.59g; Fiber 2.4g; Sugar 2.74g; Protein 2.61g

Air Fried Corn on the Cob

Prep time: 10 minutes | Cook time: 10 minutes | Serves: 4

Ingredients:

1 tablespoon vegetable oil

4 ears of corn, husks and silk removed

Unsalted butter, for topping

Salt, for topping

Freshly ground black pepper, for topping

Directions:

1. Close the lid and move SmartSwitch to AIRFRY/STOVETOP. Select AIR FRY. set temperature to 400°F, and set time to 5 minutes. Press START/STOP to begin preheating. 2. Rub the vegetable oil onto the corn, coating it thoroughly. Place the corn on the crisper tray, then place the crisper tray in the bottom of the pot. 3. Cook for 10 minutes. Flipping it halfway through the cooking time. 4. Serve with a pat of butter and a generous sprinkle of salt and pepper.

Per Serving: Calories 161; Fat 6.04g; Sodium 107mg; Carbs 27.2g; Fiber 3.9g; Sugar 4.61g; Protein 4.61g

Cheesy Broccoli Gratin

Prep time: 10 minutes | Cook time: 14 minutes | Serves: 2

Ingredients:

Olive oil spray

½ tablespoon olive oil

1 tablespoon all-purpose or gluten-free flour

⅓ cup fat-free milk

½ teaspoon ground sage

¼ teaspoon kosher salt

⅛ teaspoon freshly ground black pepper

2 cups (5 ounces) broccoli florets, roughly chopped

6 tablespoons (1½ ounces) shredded extra-sharp cheddar cheese

2 tablespoons panko bread crumbs, regular or gluten-free

1 tablespoon freshly grated Parmesan cheese

Directions:

1. Spray a round baking dish that can fit the inside of the pot with oil. 2. Combine the olive oil, flour, sage, milk, salt, and pepper in a medium bowl, stir to mix well. Add the broccoli, panko, cheddar, and Parmesan and mix well. Transfer to the baking dish. 3. Close the lid and move SmartSwitch to AIRFRY/STOVETOP. Select AIR FRY. set temperature to 330°F, and set time to 5 minutes. Press START/STOP to begin preheating. 4. Place the baking dish on the crisper tray, then place the crisper tray in the bottom of the pot. 5. Cook for 12 to 14 minutes, until the broccoli is crisp-tender and the cheese is golden brown on top. Serve immediately.

Per Serving: Calories 381; Fat 21.15g; Sodium 881mg; Carbs 29.5g; Fiber 2.5g; Sugar 4.82g; Protein 18.6g

Honey Glazed Carrots

Prep time: 10 minutes | Cook time: 12 minutes | Serves: 4

Ingredients:

3 cups baby carrots

1 tablespoon extra-virgin olive oil

1 tablespoon honey

Salt

Freshly ground black pepper

Fresh dill (optional)

Directions:

1. Close the lid and move SmartSwitch to AIRFRY/STOVETOP. Select AIR FRY. set temperature to 390°F, and set time to 5 minutes. Press START/STOP to begin preheating. 2. Mix together the carrots, honey, olive oil, salt, and pepper in a large bowl. Make sure that the carrots are thoroughly coated with oil. 3. Place the carrots on the crisper tray, then place the crisper tray in the bottom of the pot. 4. Cook for 12 minutes, or until fork-tender. 5. Once done, transfer the carrots to a bowl, sprinkle with dill, if desired, and serve.

Per Serving: Calories 64; Fat 1.7g; Sodium 232mg; Carbs 12.28g; Fiber 2.3g; Sugar 8.22g; Protein 0.8g

Simple Air Fried Cabbage

Prep time: 10 minutes | Cook time: 7 minutes | Serves: 4

Ingredients:

1 head cabbage, sliced in 1-inch-thick ribbons

1 tablespoon olive oil

1 teaspoon salt

1 teaspoon freshly ground black pepper

1 teaspoon garlic powder

1 teaspoon red pepper flakes

Directions:

1. Close the lid and move SmartSwitch to AIRFRY/STOVETOP. Select AIR FRY. set temperature to 350°F, and set time to 5 minutes. Press START/STOP to begin preheating. 2. Mix together the cabbage, olive oil, garlic powder, salt, pepper, and red pepper flakes in a large bowl. Make sure that the cabbage is thoroughly coated with oil. 3. Place the cabbage on the crisper tray, then place the crisper tray in the bottom of the pot. 4. Cook for 7 minutes. Flipping halfway through the cooking time. 5. Serve with additional salt, pepper, and/or red pepper flakes, if desired.

Per Serving: Calories 77; Fat 3.61g; Sodium 620mg; Carbs 11.11g; Fiber 3.1g; Sugar 5.48g; Protein 2.17g

Breaded Buffalo Cauliflower

Prep time: 10 minutes | Cook time: 13 minutes | Serves: 4

Ingredients:

4 tablespoons (½ stick) unsalted butter, melted

¼ cup buffalo wing sauce

4 cups cauliflower florets

1 cup panko bread crumbs

Directions:

1. Close the lid and move SmartSwitch to AIRFRY/STOVETOP. Select AIR FRY. set temperature to 350°F, and set time to 5 minutes. Press START/STOP to begin preheating. 2. Spray the crisper tray with olive oil. 3. Combine the melted butter and buffalo wing sauce in a small bowl. In another small bowl, place the panko bread crumbs. 4. Dip the cauliflower into the sauce, ensuring that the top is coated, and then dip it into the panko. 5. Place the cauliflower on the crisper tray, being careful not to overcrowd them. Then place the tray in the bottom of the pot. Spray the cauliflower generously with olive oil. 6. Cook for 7 minutes. 7. Using tongs, flip the cauliflower. Spray generously with olive oil. 8. Reset the timer and air fry for another 6 minutes.

Per Serving: Calories 234; Fat 9.56g; Sodium 418mg; Carbs 32.04g; Fiber 3.5g; Sugar 9.66g; Protein 6.27g

Sweet Potato Fries

Prep time: 10 minutes | Cook time: 20 minutes | Serves: 4

Ingredients:

2 sweet potatoes

1 teaspoon salt

½ teaspoon freshly ground black pepper

2 teaspoons olive oil

Directions:

1. Close the lid and move SmartSwitch to AIRFRY/STOVETOP. Select AIR FRY. set temperature to 380°F, and set time to 5 minutes. Press START/STOP to begin preheating. 2. Slice the sweet potatoes lengthwise into pieces that are ½ inch thick. 3. After that, take each of those slices and cut them into fries that are also ½ inch thick. 4. In a mixing bowl, combine the sweet potato fries with salt, pepper, and olive oil. 5. Make sure to coat all of the fries with oil, adding more as necessary. Place the potatoes on the crisper tray, then place the crisper tray in the bottom of the pot. 6. Air fry for 20 minutes. Stir several times during cooking so that the fries will be evenly cooked and crisp. 7. Once done, pour the potatoes into a serving bowl and toss with additional salt and pepper, if desired.

Per Serving: Calories 163; Fat 2.43g; Sodium 593mg; Carbs 32.47g; Fiber 4.2g; Sugar 1.44g; Protein 15.06g

Air Fried Sweet Potatoes

Prep time: 10 minutes | Cook time: 30 minutes | Serves: 4

Ingredients:

4 sweet potatoes

¼ cup olive oil

2 teaspoons salt

½ teaspoon freshly ground black pepper

Directions:

1. Close the lid and move SmartSwitch to AIRFRY/STOVETOP. Select AIR FRY. set temperature to 400°F, and set time to 5 minutes. Press START/STOP to begin preheating. 2. To prepare the sweet potatoes, make some holes in them using a fork and then apply a mixture of olive oil, salt, and pepper on the skins. 3. Place the coated sweet potatoes on the crisper tray, then place the crisper tray in the bottom of the pot. 4. Air fry for 30 minutes, flipping halfway through the cooking time. 5. Check to see if the sweet potatoes are fork-tender. If not, add up to 15 minutes more. (The cooking time will depend on how large the sweet potatoes are.)

Per Serving: Calories 404; Fat 13.84g; Sodium 1185mg; Carbs 64.7g; Fiber 8.2g; Sugar 2.88g; Protein 7.49g

Cheesy Hasselback Potatoes

Prep time: 10 minutes | Cook time: 35 minutes | Serves: 4

Ingredients:

4 russet potatoes

2 tablespoons olive oil

1 teaspoon salt

½ teaspoon freshly ground black pepper

¼ cup grated Parmesan cheese

Directions:

1. Close the lid and move SmartSwitch to AIRFRY/STOVETOP. Select BAKE/ROAST, set temperature to 350°F, and set time to 5 minutes. Press START/STOP to begin preheating. 2. First, slice the potatoes horizontally into half-inch wide pieces without completely cutting through the bottom so that they stay connected. 3. Then, brush olive oil over the potatoes, making sure to get the oil in between the slices, and season with salt and pepper. 4. Place the potatoes on the crisper tray, then place the crisper tray in the bottom of the pot. Bake for 20 minutes. 5. Brush more olive oil onto the potatoes. 6. Reset the timer and bake for 15 minutes more. Remove the potatoes when they are fork-tender. 7. Sprinkle the cooked potatoes with salt, pepper, and Parmesan cheese.

Per Serving: Calories 378; Fat 8.79g; Sodium 713mg; Carbs 67.74g; Fiber 4.9g; Sugar 2.29g; Protein 9.7g

Rosemary Sweet Potato Bites

Prep time: 10 minutes | Cook time: 20 minutes | Serves: 4

Ingredients:

1½ pounds small red potatoes, cut into 1-inch cubes

2 tablespoons olive oil

1 teaspoon salt

½ teaspoon freshly ground black pepper

1 tablespoon minced garlic

2 tablespoons minced fresh rosemary

Directions:

1. Close the lid and move SmartSwitch to AIRFRY/STOVETOP. Select AIR FRY. set temperature to 400°F, and set time to 5 minutes. Press START/STOP to begin preheating. 2. Mix together the diced potatoes, minced garlic, olive oil, salt, pepper, and rosemary in a bowl and toss well to coat. 3. Place the potatoes on the crisper tray, then place the crisper tray in the bottom of the pot. 4. Cook for 20 to 22 minutes. Flipping halfway through the cooking time. 5. Once done, pour the potatoes into a large serving bowl, toss with additional salt and pepper, and serve.

Per Serving: Calories 184; Fat 7.06g; Sodium 613mg; Carbs 28.12g; Fiber 3.1g; Sugar 2.22g; Protein 3.41g

Honey Cornbread

Prep time: 10 minutes | Cook time: 20 minutes | Serves: 4

Ingredients:

1 cup all-purpose flour

1 cup yellow cornmeal

½ cup sugar

1 teaspoon salt

2 teaspoons baking powder

1 large egg

1 cup milk

⅓ cup vegetable oil

¼ cup honey

Directions:

1. Close the lid and move SmartSwitch to AIRFRY/STOVETOP. Select BAKE/ROAST, set temperature to 360°F, and set time to 5 minutes. Press START/STOP to begin preheating. 2. Spray an air fryer–safe baking pan with olive oil or cooking spray. 3. Mix together the flour, cornmeal, sugar, baking powder, egg, salt, milk, oil, and honey in a mixing bowl. 4. Pour the cornbread batter into the prepared pan. Place the pan on the crisper tray, then place the crisper tray in the bottom of the pot. Bake for 20 minutes. 5. To check if the center of the cornbread is cooked, put a toothpick in it. If it's not fully cooked, bake for another 3 to 4 minutes. 6. After that, take the pan out of the air fryer using silicone oven mitts and let it cool down a bit. Finally, serve it while it's still warm.

Per Serving: Calories 580; Fat 22.1g; Sodium 616mg; Carbs 89.21g; Fiber 2.5g; Sugar 33.46g; Protein 8.68g

Cheese Tomato-Spinach Stuffed Mushrooms

Prep time: 10 minutes | Cook time: 12 minutes | Serves: 4

Ingredients:

4 large portobello mushroom caps (about 3 ounces each)

Olive oil spray

Kosher salt

2 medium plum tomatoes, chopped

1 cup baby spinach, roughly chopped

¾ cup crumbled feta cheese

1 shallot, chopped

1 large garlic clove, minced

¼ cup chopped fresh basil

2 tablespoons panko bread crumbs, regular or gluten-free

1 tablespoon chopped fresh oregano

1 tablespoon freshly grated Parmesan cheese

⅛ teaspoon freshly ground black pepper

1 tablespoon olive oil

Balsamic glaze (optional), for drizzling

Directions:

1. First, remove the black gills from each mushroom cap using a small metal spoon. 2. Then, spray both sides of the mushrooms with olive oil and add a pinch of salt. 3. In a medium-sized bowl, mix together tomatoes, spinach, feta, shallot, garlic, basil, panko, oregano, Parmesan, ¼ teaspoon salt, pepper, and olive oil. Stir everything well. 4. Fill each mushroom cap with the mixture, taking care not to spill any. 5. Close the lid and move SmartSwitch to AIRFRY/STOVETOP. Select AIR FRY. set temperature to 370°F, and set time to 5 minutes. Press START/STOP to begin preheating. 6. Working in batches, arrange a single layer of the stuffed mushrooms on the crisper tray, then place the crisper tray in the bottom of the pot. Cook for 10 to 12 minutes, until the mushrooms are tender and the top is golden. 7. Use a flexible spatula to carefully remove the mushrooms from the pot and transfer to a serving dish. 8. Drizzle the balsamic glaze (if using) over the mushrooms and serve.

Per Serving: Calories 207; Fat 10.69g; Sodium 482mg; Carbs 21.25g; Fiber 2.5g; Sugar 8.29g; Protein 7.9g

Parmesan Broccoli

Prep time: 10 minutes | Cook time: 4 minutes | Serves: 4

Ingredients:

1-pound broccoli florets

2 teaspoons minced garlic

2 tablespoons olive oil

¼ cup grated or shaved Parmesan cheese

Directions:

1. Close the lid and move SmartSwitch to AIRFRY/STOVETOP. Select AIR FRY. set temperature to 360°F, and set time to 5 minutes. Press START/STOP to begin preheating. 2. In a small mixing bowl, combine the broccoli florets, olive oil, garlic, and Parmesan cheese. 3. Place the broccoli on the crisper tray, then place the crisper tray in the bottom of the pot. Cook for 4 minutes. Serve warm.

Per Serving: Calories 113; Fat 9.05g; Sodium 151mg; Carbs 4.56g; Fiber 3.1g; Sugar 0.45g; Protein 5.46g

Teriyaki Tofu "Steaks"

Prep time: 15 minutes | Cook time: 10 minutes | Serves: 2

Ingredients:

Tofu:

7 ounces extra-firm tofu (about ½ block), drained and cut into 4 (½-inch-thick) slices

2 tablespoons reduced-sodium soy sauce* or tamari

1 teaspoon toasted sesame oil

1 teaspoon unseasoned rice vinegar

1 teaspoon light brown sugar

1 garlic clove, grated

½ teaspoon grated fresh ginger

⅓ cup white and black sesame seeds

1 large egg

Olive oil spray

Sriracha Mayo:

4 teaspoons mayonnaise

1 teaspoon Sriracha sauce

1 scallion, chopped, for garnish (optional)

Directions:

1. To prepare the tofu, first place the tofu slices on a kitchen towel. Cover the slices with another towel and press lightly to remove the excess water. 2. After that, transfer the tofu to a shallow bowl or baking dish that is large enough to accommodate the tofu in a single layer. 3. In a small bowl, whisk together soy sauce, sesame oil, brown sugar, vinegar, garlic, and ginger. 4. Next, pour half of the marinade over the tofu, flip it over and pour the remaining marinade on the other side. 5. Allow the tofu to marinate in the refrigerator for at least one hour or overnight. 6. Place the sesame seeds on a small plate or pie dish. 7. In another small dish or bowl, beat the egg. 8. Remove each tofu slice from the marinade, allowing the excess to drip off, then dip in the egg. 9. Using a fork, dip in the sesame seeds, coating each side. 10. Transfer to a work surface. Spray one side with olive oil, then gently flip and spray the other side. (Discard the excess marinade.)11. Close the lid of your Ninja Speedi Rapid Cooker & Air Fryer and flip the SmartSwitch to AIRFRY/STOVETOP. Select AIR FRY. set temperature to 400°F, and set time to 5 minutes. Press START/STOP to begin preheating. 12. Working in batches, arrange a single layer of the tofu on the crisper tray, then place the crisper tray in the bottom of the pot. Cook for about 10 minutes, flipping halfway through the cooking time, until toasted and crisp. 13. Meanwhile, for the Sriracha mayo: In a small bowl, combine the mayonnaise and Sriracha. 14. To serve, top each tofu "steak" with the Sriracha mayo and some scallion (if using).

Per Serving: Calories 349; Fat 28.65g; Sodium 1127mg; Carbs 9.55g; Fiber 3.6g; Sugar 3.42g; Protein 18.86g

Crispy Cauliflower Nuggets

Prep time: 10 minutes | Cook time: 8 minutes | Serves: 4

Ingredients:

3 large eggs, beaten

½ cup all-purpose or gluten-free flour

28 bite-size (about 1½-inch) cauliflower florets (16 ounces)

Olive oil spray

6 tablespoons Frank's Red Hot sauce

1 tablespoon unsalted butter, melted

Blue cheese dip, homemade or store-bought (optional)

Carrot sticks and celery sticks, for serving (optional)

Directions:

1. Close the lid and move SmartSwitch to AIRFRY/STOVETOP. Select AIR FRY. set temperature to 380°F, and set time to 5 minutes. Press START/STOP to begin preheating. 2. Put the eggs in a small bowl and the flour in a medium-sized bowl. Then, take the cauliflower and dip it into the egg, followed by the flour to cover it completely. 3. Shake off any extra flour and place the coated cauliflower on a work surface. 4. Spray oil on both sides of the cauliflower. Working in batches, arrange a single layer of the cauliflower on the crisper tray, then place the crisper tray in the bottom of the pot. Cook for 7 to 8 minutes, flipping halfway through the cooking time, until golden and tender. 5. When all the batches are done, return all the cauliflower to the air fryer and cook for 1 minute to heat through. 6. Transfer to a large bowl and toss with the hot sauce and melted butter. 7. If desired, serve with blue cheese dressing and vegetable sticks.

Per Serving: Calories 172; Fat 6.41g; Sodium 73mg; Carbs 23.12g; Fiber 4.5g; Sugar 4.48g; Protein 7.76g

Sweet Acorn Squash

Prep time: 10 minutes | Cook time: 15 minutes | Serves: 2

Ingredients:

1 teaspoon coconut oil

1 medium acorn squash, halved crosswise and seeded

1 teaspoon light brown sugar

Few dashes of ground nutmeg

Few dashes of ground cinnamon

Directions:

1. Apply coconut oil onto the sliced parts of the squash and then evenly distribute brown sugar, nutmeg, and cinnamon over it. 2. Close the lid and move SmartSwitch to AIRFRY/STOVETOP. Select AIR FRY. set temperature to 350°F, and set time to 5 minutes. Press START/STOP to begin preheating. 3. Place the squash halves, cut sides up, on the crisper tray, then place the crisper tray in the bottom of the pot. Cook for 15 minutes, until soft in the center when pierced with a paring knife. Serve immediately.

Per Serving: Calories 115; Fat 2.52g; Sodium 7mg; Carbs 24.91g; Fiber 3.3g; Sugar 2.24g; Protein 1.74g

Mexican Street Corn Kernels

Prep time: 10 minutes | Cook time: 7 minutes | Serves: 4

Ingredients:

4 medium ears corn, husked

Olive oil spray

2 tablespoons mayonnaise

1 tablespoon fresh lime juice

½ teaspoon ancho chile powder

¼ teaspoon kosher salt

2 ounces crumbled Cotija or feta cheese

2 tablespoons chopped fresh cilantro

Directions:

1. Close the lid and move SmartSwitch to AIRFRY/STOVETOP. Select AIR FRY. set temperature to 375°F, and set time to 5 minutes. Press START/STOP to begin preheating. 2. Spray the corn with olive oil. Working in batches, arrange the ears of corn on the crisper tray in a single layer, then place the tray in the bottom of the pot. Cook for about 7 minutes, flipping halfway through the cooking time, until the kernels are tender when pierced with a paring knife. 3. When cool enough to handle, cut the corn kernels off the cob. 4. Add mayonnaise, lime juice, ancho powder, and salt to a large bowl and stir to mix well. Add the corn kernels and mix to combine. 5. Transfer to a serving dish and top with the Cotija and cilantro. Serve right away.

Per Serving: Calories 186; Fat 7.1g; Sodium 355mg; Carbs 28.41g; Fiber 4g; Sugar 5.36g; Protein 7.1g

Charred Green Beans

Prep time: 10 minutes | Cook time: 8 minutes | Serves: 4

Ingredients:

1 tablespoon reduced-sodium soy sauce or tamari

½ tablespoon Sriracha sauce

4 teaspoons toasted sesame oil

12 ounces trimmed green beans

½ tablespoon toasted sesame seeds

Directions:

1. Mix the soy sauce, Sriracha, and 1 teaspoon of sesame oil in a small bowl. In a big bowl, put the green beans and mix with the remaining 3 teaspoons of sesame oil until the beans are coated. 2. Close the lid and move SmartSwitch to AIRFRY/STOVETOP. Select AIR FRY. set temperature to 375°F, and set time to 5 minutes. Press START/STOP to begin preheating. 3. Working in batches, arrange a single layer of the green beans on the crisper tray, then place the crisper tray in the bottom of the pot. 4. Cook for about 8 minutes, flipping halfway through the cooking time, until charred and tender. Transfer to a serving dish. 5. Toss with the sauce and sesame seeds and serve.

Per Serving: Calories 68; Fat 5.38g; Sodium 275mg; Carbs 4.34g; Fiber 1.9g; Sugar 0.83g; Protein 1.63g

Bacon-Wrapped Asparagus

Prep time: 10 minutes | Cook time: 10 minutes | Serves: 4

Ingredients:

20 asparagus spears (12 ounces), tough ends trimmed

Olive oil spray

½ teaspoon grated lemon zest

⅛ teaspoon kosher salt

Freshly ground black pepper

4 slices center-cut bacon

Directions:

1. Place the asparagus on a small sheet pan and spritz with olive oil. Add lemon zest, salt, and pepper to taste, and mix well to coat the asparagus. 2. Divide the asparagus into four groups, with each group consisting of five spears, and then wrap the center of each group with a slice of bacon. 3. Close the lid and move SmartSwitch to AIRFRY/STOVETOP. Select AIR FRY. set temperature to 400°F, and set time to 5 minutes. Press START/STOP to begin preheating. 4. Working in batches, place the asparagus bundles on the crisper tray, then place the crisper tray in the bottom of the pot. 5. Cook until the bacon is browned and the asparagus is slightly charred on the edges, 8 to 10 minutes, depending on the thickness of the spears. Serve immediately.

Per Serving: Calories 110; Fat 10.24g; Sodium 200mg; Carbs 0.99g; Fiber 0.4g; Sugar 0.56g; Protein 3.65g

Classic French Fries

Prep time: 10 minutes | Cook time: 15 minutes | Serves: 2

Ingredients:

2 (6-ounce) Yukon Gold or russet potatoes, washed and dried

2 teaspoons olive oil

¼ teaspoon kosher salt

¼ teaspoon garlic powder

Freshly ground black pepper

Directions:

1. Slice the potatoes into ¼-inch-thick pieces lengthwise, and then cut each slice into ¼-inch-thick fries. 2. After that, put the potatoes into a medium bowl and mix them with oil. 3. Add salt, garlic powder, and pepper as per your taste and mix well. 4. Close the lid and move SmartSwitch to AIRFRY/STOVETOP. Select AIR FRY. set temperature to 350°F, and set time to 5 minutes. Press START/STOP to begin preheating. 5. Working in batches, arrange a single layer (no overlapping) of the potatoes on the crisper tray, then place the crisper tray in the bottom of the pot. 6. Cook for 12 to 15 minutes, flipping halfway, until the potatoes are golden and crisp. Serve immediately.

Per Serving: Calories 346; Fat 8.41g; Sodium 1633mg; Carbs 63.26g; Fiber 7.4g; Sugar 0.01g; Protein 6.69g

Kale Sushi Roll

Prep time: 15 minutes | Cook time: 10 minutes | Serves: 12

Ingredients:

Kale Salad:

1 tbsp. sesame seeds

¾ tsp. soy sauce

¼ tsp. ginger

⅛ tsp. garlic powder

¾ tsp. toasted sesame oil

½ tsp. rice vinegar

1½ cup chopped kale

Sushi Rolls:

½ of a sliced avocado

3 sheets of sushi nori

1 batch cauliflower rice

Sriracha Mayo:

Sriracha sauce

¼ cup vegan mayo

Coating:

½ cup panko breadcrumbs

Directions:

1. Mix all the ingredients of the kale salad together and keep it aside. 2. Take a sheet of nori, spread a handful of rice on it, then add 2-3 tablespoons of kale salad and avocado. 3. Roll it up to make sushi. For the mayo, whisk all the mayo ingredients together until smooth. 4. Close the lid and move SmartSwitch to AIRFRY/STOVETOP. Select AIR FRY. set temperature to 390°F, and set time to 5 minutes. Press START/STOP to begin preheating. 5. Add breadcrumbs to a bowl. Coat sushi rolls in crumbs till coated and place on the crisper tray, then place the crisper tray in the bottom of the pot. 6. Cook the rolls for 10 minutes, stir gently at 5 minutes. 7. Slice each roll into 6-8 pieces and serve with the mayo!

Per Serving: Calories 66; Fat 3.91g; Sodium 137mg; Carbs 6.78g; Fiber 1.4g; Sugar 1.4g; Protein 1.55g

Chapter 3 Poultry Recipes

Gingered Chicken with Cilantro Lemon Sauce

Prep time: 10 minutes | Cook time: 20 minutes | Serves: 4

Ingredients:

2 tablespoons spring onions, minced

1 tablespoon ginger, grated

4 garlic cloves, minced

2 tablespoons coconut aminos

8 chicken drumsticks

½ cup chicken stock

Salt and black pepper to the taste

1 teaspoon olive oil

¼ cup cilantro, chopped

1 tablespoon lemon juice

Directions:

1. Start by heating up a frying pan with oil on medium-high heat. Then, place the chicken drumsticks in the pan and cook them for 2 minutes on each side until they are browned. 2. After that, transfer the drumsticks to a pan that fits the pot. Add all the other ingredients, toss everything, put the pan on the crisper tray, then place the crisper tray in the bottom of the pot. 3. Close the lid and move SmartSwitch to AIRFRY/STOVETOP. Select AIR FRY, set temperature to 370°F, and set time to 20 minutes. Press START/STOP to begin cooking. 4. Divide the chicken and lemon sauce between plates and serve.

Per Serving: Calories 453; Fat 25.49g; Sodium 329mg; Carbs 4.47g; Fiber 0.5g; Sugar 1.47g; Protein 48.35g

Cheese Chicken Quesadilla

Prep time: 15 minutes | Cook time: 5 minutes | Serves: 2

Ingredients:

2 low carb tortillas

7 oz. chicken breast, skinless, boneless, boiled

1 tablespoon cream cheese

1 teaspoon butter, melted

Cooking spray

1 teaspoon minced garlic

1 teaspoon fresh dill, chopped

½ teaspoon salt

2 oz. Monterey Jack cheese, shredded

Directions:

1. Using a fork, tear apart the chicken breast and place it in a bowl. 2. Then, add cream cheese, butter, minced garlic, dill, and salt. Finally, mix in the shredded Monterey jack cheese with the shredded chicken. 3. Then put 1 tortilla in a baking pan that can fit the pot. 4. Top it with the shredded chicken mixture and cover with the second corn tortilla. 5. Place the pan on the crisper tray, then place the crisper tray in the bottom of the pot. Close the lid and move SmartSwitch to AIRFRY/STOVETOP. Select AIR FRY. set temperature to 400°F, and set time to 5 minutes. Press START/STOP to begin cooking. 6. Serve warm.

Per Serving: Calories 373; Fat 22.66g; Sodium 873mg; Carbs 12.21g; Fiber 1.8g; Sugar 0.63g; Protein 29.81g

Mozzarella and Spinach Stuffed Chicken

Prep time: 10 minutes | Cook time: 24 minutes | Serves: 6

Ingredients:

6 chicken breasts, skinless, boneless and halved

A pinch of salt and black pepper

2 tablespoons olive oil

1-pound mozzarella, sliced

2 cups baby spinach

1 teaspoon Italian seasoning

2 tomatoes, sliced

1 tablespoon basil, chopped

Directions:

1. Close the lid and move SmartSwitch to AIRFRY/STOVETOP. Select AIR FRY. set temperature to 370°F, and set time to 5 minutes. Press START/STOP to begin preheating. 2. Make slits in each chicken breast halves, season with salt, pepper and Italian seasoning and stuff with mozzarella, spinach and tomatoes. 3. Drizzle the oil over the stuffed chicken, put it on the crisper tray, then place the crisper tray in the bottom of the pot. 4. Cook for 12 minutes per side. Divide between plates and serve with basil sprinkled on top.

Per Serving: Calories 653; Fat 31.39g; Sodium 788mg; Carbs 4.21g; Fiber 1.8g; Sugar 1.73g; Protein 84.95g

Simple Air Fried Turkey Bacon

Prep time: 10 minutes | Cook time: 8 minutes | Serves: 2

Ingredients:

7 oz. turkey bacon

1 teaspoon coconut oil, melted

½ teaspoon ground black pepper

Directions:

1. Close the lid and move SmartSwitch to AIRFRY/STOVETOP. Select AIR FRY. set temperature to 350°F, and set time to 5 minutes. Press START/STOP to begin preheating. 2. Slice the turkey bacon and sprinkle it with ground black pepper and coconut oil. 3. Arrange the turkey bacon on the crisper tray, then place the crisper tray in the bottom of the pot. Cook it for 4 minutes. 4. Then flip the bacon on another side and cook for 4 minutes more.

Per Serving: Calories 332; Fat 31.57g; Sodium 1455mg; Carbs 7.34g; Fiber 2.7g; Sugar 0.57g; Protein 10.82g

Lime Hot Chicken Wings

Prep time: 10 minutes | Cook time: 30 minutes | Serves: 4

Ingredients:

1 tablespoon olive oil

2 pounds chicken wings

1 tablespoon lime juice

2 teaspoons smoked paprika

1 teaspoon red pepper flakes, crushed

Salt and black pepper to the taste

Directions:

1. Close the lid and move SmartSwitch to AIRFRY/STOVETOP. Select AIR FRY. set temperature to 380°F, and set time to 5 minutes. Press START/STOP to begin preheating. 2. In a bowl, mix the chicken wings with all the other ingredients and toss well. 3. Put the chicken wings on the crisper tray, then place the crisper tray in the bottom of the pot. Cook for 15 minutes per side. 4. Divide between plates and serve with a side salad.

Per Serving: Calories 325; Fat 11.58g; Sodium 185mg; Carbs 2.05g; Fiber 0.6g; Sugar 0.79g; Protein 50.24g

Air Fried Paprika Duck Skin

Prep time: 10 minutes | Cook time: 28 minutes | Serves: 6

Ingredients:

10 oz. duck skin

1 teaspoon sunflower oil

½ teaspoon salt

½ teaspoon ground paprika

Directions:

1. Close the lid and move SmartSwitch to AIRFRY/STOVETOP. Select AIR FRY. set temperature to 375°F, and set time to 5 minutes. Press START/STOP to begin preheating. 2. Then sprinkle the duck skin with sunflower oil, salt, and ground paprika. 3. Put the duck skin on the crisper tray, then place the crisper tray in the bottom of the pot. Cook for 18 minutes. 4. Then flip it on another side and cook for 10 minutes more or until it is crunchy from both sides.

Per Serving: Calories 107; Fat 7.96g; Sodium 220mg; Carbs 0.11g; Fiber 0.1g; Sugar 0.02g; Protein 8.26g

Coconut Chicken Tenders

Prep time: 10 minutes | Cook time: 20 minutes | Serves: 4

Ingredients:

4 chicken breasts, skinless, boneless and cut into tenders

A pinch of salt and black pepper

⅓ cup almond flour

2 eggs, whisked

9 ounces coconut flakes

Directions:

1. Close the lid and move SmartSwitch to AIRFRY/STOVETOP. Select AIR FRY. set temperature to 400°F, and set time to 5 minutes. Press START/STOP to begin preheating. 2. First, add salt and pepper to the chicken tenders. Then, coat them with almond flour and dip them in eggs. 3. Finally, cover them in coconut flakes. Put the chicken tenders on the crisper tray, then place the crisper tray in the bottom of the pot. Cook for 10 minutes per side. 4. Divide between plates and serve with a side salad.

Per Serving: Calories 366; Fat 11.16g; Sodium 246mg; Carbs 3.96g; Fiber 0.9g; Sugar 2.57g; Protein 58.54g

Spicy Chicken Cutlets

Prep time: 10 minutes | Cook time: 16 minutes | Serves: 4

Ingredients:

15 oz. chicken fillet

1 teaspoon white pepper

1 teaspoon ghee, melted

½ teaspoon onion powder

¼ teaspoon chili flakes

Directions:

1. Close the lid and move SmartSwitch to AIRFRY/STOVETOP. Select AIR FRY. set temperature to 365°F, and set time to 5 minutes. Press START/STOP to begin preheating. 2. Cut the chicken fillet into small pieces and season it with white pepper, onion powder, and chili flakes. Mix everything together until it's well combined. 3. Shape the mixture into medium-sized cutlets. 4. Brush the crisper tray with ghee and put the chicken cutlets on the tray, then place the tray in the bottom of the pot. 5. Cook for 8 minutes and then flip on another side with the help of the spatula, cook for 8 minutes more. 6. Transfer the cooked chicken cutlets on the serving plate.

Per Serving: Calories 164; Fat 9.61g; Sodium 77mg; Carbs 0.78g; Fiber 0.3g; Sugar 0.03g; Protein 18.67g

Tomato Sauce-Glazed Chicken Drumsticks

Prep time: 10 minutes | Cook time: 30 minutes | Serves: 4

Ingredients:

1 and ½ cups Keto tomato sauce

1 teaspoon onion powder

A pinch of salt and black pepper

1 tablespoon coconut aminos

½ teaspoon chili powder

2 pounds chicken drumsticks

Directions:

1. In bowl, mix the chicken drumsticks with all the other ingredients, toss and keep in the fridge for 10 minutes. 2. Close the lid and move SmartSwitch to AIRFRY/STOVETOP. Select AIR FRY. set temperature to 380°F, and set time to 5 minutes. Press START/STOP to begin preheating. 3. Drain the drumsticks, put them on the crisper tray, then place the crisper tray in the bottom of the pot. Cook for 15 minutes per side. 4. Divide everything between plates and serve.

Per Serving: Calories 388; Fat 21.14g; Sodium 262mg; Carbs 5.35g; Fiber 1.3g; Sugar 2.92g; Protein 42.1g

Celery Chicken Thighs

Prep time: 10 minutes | Cook time: 15 minutes | Serves: 4

Ingredients:

16 oz. chicken thighs, skinless

1 teaspoon ground celery root

1 teaspoon dried celery leaves

1 teaspoon apple cider vinegar

½ teaspoon salt

1 tablespoon sunflower oil

Directions:

1. First, apply a mixture of celery root, dried celery leaves, and salt to the chicken thighs and rub them well. 2. Afterwards, add apple cider vinegar and sunflower oil to the chicken by sprinkling it over the surface. Leave it for 15 minutes to marinate. 3. After this, Close the lid and move SmartSwitch to AIRFRY/STOVETOP. Select AIR FRY. set temperature to 385°F, and set time to 5 minutes. Press START/STOP to begin preheating. 4. Put the chicken thighs on the crisper tray, then place the crisper tray in the bottom of the pot. Cook them for 12 minutes. 5. Then flip the chicken on another side and cook for 3 minutes more. 6. Transfer the cooked chicken thighs on the plate.

Per Serving: Calories 282; Fat 22.34g; Sodium 384mg; Carbs 0.33g; Fiber 0g; Sugar 0.02g; Protein 18.74g

Air Fried Cinnamon Chicken Thighs

Prep time: 10 minutes | Cook time: 30 minutes | Serves: 4

Ingredients:

2 pounds chicken thighs

A pinch of salt and black pepper

2 tablespoons olive oil

½ teaspoon cinnamon, ground

Directions:

1. Close the lid and move SmartSwitch to AIRFRY/STOVETOP. Select AIR FRY. set temperature to 360°F, and set time to 5 minutes. Press START/STOP to begin preheating. 2. Season the chicken thighs with salt and pepper, and rub with the rest of the ingredients. 3. Put the chicken thighs on the crisper tray, then place the crisper tray in the bottom of the pot, cook for 15 minutes per side, divide between plates and serve.

Per Serving: Calories 566; Fat 44.45g; Sodium 185mg; Carbs 1.89g; Fiber 0.3g; Sugar 0.58g; Protein 37.71g

Spicy Chicken Wings

Prep time: 10 minutes | Cook time: 12 minutes | Serves: 6

Ingredients:

1-pound chicken wings

1 teaspoon ground paprika

1 teaspoon chili powder

½ teaspoon salt

1 tablespoon sunflower oil

Directions:

1. Close the lid and move SmartSwitch to AIRFRY/STOVETOP. Select AIR FRY. set temperature to 400°F, and set time to 5 minutes. Press START/STOP to begin preheating. 2. First, pour some sunflower oil into a shallow bowl. 3. Then, add chili powder and ground paprika to the oil and stir the mixture gently. 4. Finally, sprinkle the chicken wings with the red chili mixture and some salt. 5. Place the chicken wings on the crisper tray in one layer, then place the tray in the bottom of the pot. Cook for 6 minutes. 6. Then flip the wings on another side and cook for additional 6 minutes.

Per Serving: Calories 118; Fat 5.12g; Sodium 268mg; Carbs 0.43g; Fiber 0.3g; Sugar 0.07g; Protein 16.72g

Lemon Chicken with Chives

Prep time: 10 minutes | Cook time: 20 minutes | Serves: 4

Ingredients:

1-pound chicken tenders, boneless, skinless

A pinch of salt and black pepper

Juice of 1 lemon

1 tablespoon chives, chopped

A drizzle of olive oil

Directions:

1. Close the lid and move SmartSwitch to AIRFRY/STOVETOP. Select AIR FRY. set temperature to 370°F, and set time to 5 minutes. Press START/STOP to begin preheating. 2. In a bowl, combine the chicken tenders with all ingredients except the chives, toss well, put the meat on the crisper tray, then place the crisper tray in the bottom of the pot. 3. Cook for 10 minutes per side. Divide between plates and serve with chives sprinkled on top.

Per Serving: Calories 143; Fat 4.24g; Sodium 86mg; Carbs 1.92g; Fiber 0.2g; Sugar 0.89g; Protein 23.35g

Turmeric Chicken Wings

Prep time: 10 minutes | Cook time: 15 minutes | Serves: 8

Ingredients:

8 chicken wings

1 teaspoon Splenda

1 teaspoon ground turmeric

½ teaspoon cayenne pepper

1 tablespoon avocado oil

Directions:

1. Close the lid and move SmartSwitch to AIRFRY/STOVETOP. Select AIR FRY. set temperature to 390°F, and set time to 5 minutes. Press START/STOP to begin preheating. 2. Combine Splenda and avocado oil and mix until the Splenda dissolves. 3. Next, season the chicken wings with ground turmeric and cayenne pepper. 4. Finally, brush both sides of the chicken wings with the sweet avocado oil. 5. Place the chicken wings on the crisper tray, then place the crisper tray in the bottom of the pot. Cook them for 15 minutes. Serve warm.

Per Serving: Calories 56; Fat 2.81g; Sodium 24mg; Carbs 0.89g; Fiber 0.1g; Sugar 0.53g; Protein 6.42g

Red Vinegar Marinated Chicken Wings

Prep time: 10 minutes | Cook time: 30 minutes | Serves: 6

Ingredients:

2 pounds chicken wings, halved

¼ cup red vinegar

4 garlic cloves, minced

Salt and black pepper to the taste

4 tablespoons olive oil

1 tablespoon garlic powder

1 teaspoon turmeric powder

Directions:

1. In a bowl, mix the chicken with all the other ingredients and toss well. Chill for 20 minutes. 2. Close the lid and move SmartSwitch to AIRFRY/STOVETOP. Select AIR FRY. set temperature to 370°F, and set time to 5 minutes. Press START/STOP to begin preheating. 3. Put the chicken wings on the crisper tray, then place the crisper tray in the bottom of the pot. Cook for 30 minutes, flipping halfway through the cooking time. 4. Divide everything between plates and serve with a side salad.

Per Serving: Calories 285; Fat 14.41g; Sodium 125mg; Carbs 2.91g; Fiber 0.4g; Sugar 0.46g; Protein 33.82g

Herbed Lemon Chicken Drumsticks

Prep time: 10 minutes | Cook time: 21 minutes | Serves: 4

Ingredients:

4 chicken drumsticks, with skin, bone-in

1 teaspoon dried cilantro

½ teaspoon dried oregano

½ teaspoon salt

1 teaspoon lemon juice

1 teaspoon butter, softened

2 garlic cloves, diced

Directions:

1. Close the lid and move SmartSwitch to AIRFRY/STOVETOP. Select AIR FRY. set temperature to 375°F, and set time to 5 minutes. Press START/STOP to begin preheating. 2. In the mixing bowl mix up dried cilantro, oregano, and salt. Then fill the chicken drumstick's skin with a cilantro mixture. Add butter and diced garlic. Sprinkle the chicken with lemon juice. 3. Put the chicken drumsticks on the crisper tray, then place the crisper tray in the bottom of the pot. 4. Cook them for 21 minutes.

Per Serving: Calories 221; Fat 12.93g; Sodium 436mg; Carbs 0.82g; Fiber 0.1g; Sugar 0.05g; Protein 23.63g

Herbed Turkey Breasts with Celery

Prep time: 10 minutes | Cook time: 25 minutes | Serves: 4

Ingredients:

2 turkey breasts, skinless, boneless and halved

4 tablespoons butter, melted

2 tablespoons thyme, chopped

2 tablespoons sage, chopped

1 tablespoons rosemary, chopped

2 tablespoons parsley, chopped

A pinch of salt and black pepper

2 cups chicken stock

2 celery stalks, chopped

Directions:

1. First, put some butter in a pan that is the right size for your air fryer, and heat it on medium-high heat. 2. Then, add the turkey to the pan and cook it for 2-3 minutes on each side until it turns brown. 3. After that, add the herbs, stock, celery, salt, and pepper to the pan and mix them together. 4. Close the lid and move SmartSwitch to AIRFRY/STOVETOP. Select AIR FRY. set temperature to 390°F, and set time to 5 minutes. Press START/STOP to begin preheating. 5. Put the pan on the crisper tray, then place the crisper tray in the bottom of the pot. Cook for 20 minutes. Divide between plates and serve.

Per Serving: Calories 167; Fat 13.36g; Sodium 369mg; Carbs 7.11g; Fiber 1.1g; Sugar 2.99g; Protein 5.46g

Tasty Onion and Cayenne Chicken Tenders

Prep time: 10 minutes | Cook time: 10 minutes | Serves: 2

Ingredients:

8 oz. chicken fillet

1 teaspoon minced onion

¼ teaspoon onion powder

¼ teaspoon salt

½ teaspoon cayenne pepper

Cooking spray

Directions:

1. Close the lid and move SmartSwitch to AIRFRY/STOVETOP. Select AIR FRY. set temperature to 365°F, and set time to 5 minutes. Press START/STOP to begin preheating. 2. Cut the chicken fillet into 2 tenders and sprinkle with salt, onion powder, and cayenne pepper. 3. Spray the crisper tray with cooking spray and place the chicken tenders on the crisper tray, top the chicken with minced onion. 4. Then place the tray in the bottom of the pot. Cook for 10 minutes. Serve warm.

Per Serving: Calories 218; Fat 9.4g; Sodium 372mg; Carbs 13.03g; Fiber 1.7g; Sugar 8.37g; Protein 21.19g

Rosemary Butter Turkey Breasts

Prep time: 10 minutes | Cook time: 24 minutes | Serves: 4

Ingredients:

1 turkey breast, skinless, boneless and cut into 4 pieces

A pinch of salt and black pepper

Juice of 1 lemon

2 tablespoons rosemary, chopped

2 tablespoons butter, melted

Directions:

1. Close the lid and move SmartSwitch to AIRFRY/STOVETOP. Select AIR FRY. set temperature to 380°F, and set time to 5 minutes. Press START/STOP to begin preheating. 2. Mix together the butter, rosemary, lemon juice, salt and pepper in a bowl. 3. Brush the turkey pieces with the rosemary butter, put them on the crisper tray, then place the crisper tray in the bottom of the pot. 4. Cook for 12 minutes per side. Divide between plates and serve with a side salad.

Per Serving: Calories 81; Fat 6.21g; Sodium 242mg; Carbs 2.96g; Fiber 0.4g; Sugar 1.62g; Protein 3.94g

Spinach & Celery Stuffed Chicken Rolls

Prep time: 10 minutes | Cook time: 25 minutes | Serves: 5

Ingredients:

1-pound chicken fillet

2 oz. celery stalk, chopped

¼ teaspoon ground paprika

¼ teaspoon ground nutmeg

½ teaspoon garlic powder

1 teaspoon ghee, melted

½ teaspoon salt

1 teaspoon dried oregano

1 teaspoon cream cheese

1 teaspoon avocado oil

1 cup spinach, chopped

Directions:

1. Cut the chicken fillet into 5 pieces and beat them gently with the help of the kitchen hammer. You should get 5 flat chicken fillets. 2. Season the chicken with paprika, garlic powder, nutmeg, salt, and oregano. 3. Cook it in a skillet with ghee for 1-2 minutes on medium heat, and then add spinach and cream cheese. Add chopped celery and cook the greens on low heat for 10 minutes. 4. Drain the liquid from the spinach and spoon the cooked greens onto the chicken fillets. 5. Roll the chicken into rolls and secure them with toothpicks or kitchen thread, if necessary. 6. Close the lid and move SmartSwitch to AIRFRY/STOVETOP. Select AIR FRY. set temperature to 375°F, and set time to 5 minutes. Press START/STOP to begin preheating. 7. Put the chicken rolls on the crisper tray and sprinkle with avocado oil. Then place the tray in the bottom of the pot. 8. Cook the rolls for 12 minutes. Serve warm.

Per Serving: Calories 124; Fat 4.51g; Sodium 325mg; Carbs 1.08g; Fiber 0.5g; Sugar 0.24g; Protein 18.87g

Paprika Turkey Breast and Shallot Sauce

Prep time: 10 minutes | Cook time: 30 minutes | Serves: 4

Ingredients:

1 big turkey breast, skinless, boneless and cubed

1 tablespoon olive oil

¼ teaspoon sweet paprika

Salt and black pepper to the taste

1 cup chicken stock

3 tablespoons butter, melted

4 shallots, chopped

Directions:

1. Begin by heating a frying pan of appropriate size for the air fryer on medium-high heat, with both olive oil and butter. 2. Then, add the turkey cubes and cook for three minutes on each side until browned. 3. Afterward, include the shallots and stir while sautéing for another five minutes. 4. Add the paprika, stock, salt, and pepper, and toss everything together. 5. Flip the SmartSwitch to AIRFRY/STOVETOP. Select AIR FRY. set temperature to 370°F, and set time to 5 minutes. Press START/STOP to begin preheating. 6. Place the pan on the crisper tray, then place the crisper tray in the bottom of the pot. 7. Cook for 20 minutes. Divide into bowls and serve.

Per Serving: Calories 365; Fat 15.97g; Sodium 308mg; Carbs 4.95g; Fiber 0.5g; Sugar 2.33g; Protein 48.2g

Bacon Wrapped Chicken

Prep time: 10 minutes | Cook time: 25 minutes | Serves: 2

Ingredients:

2 chicken legs

4 oz. bacon, sliced

½ teaspoon salt

½ teaspoon ground black pepper

1 teaspoon sesame oil

Directions:

1. Close the lid and move SmartSwitch to AIRFRY/STOVETOP. Select AIR FRY. set temperature to 385°F, and set time to 5 minutes. Press START/STOP to begin preheating. 2. Sprinkle the chicken legs with salt and ground black pepper and wrap in the sliced bacon. 3. Put the chicken legs on the crisper tray and sprinkle with sesame oil, then place the tray in the bottom of the pot. 4. Cook the bacon chicken legs for 25 minutes.

Per Serving: Calories 259; Fat 15.1g; Sodium 834mg; Carbs 2.32g; Fiber 0.8g; Sugar 0.29g; Protein 28.53g

Chapter 4 Beef, Pork, and Lamb Recipes

Worcestershire Sauce Glazed Ribeye Steaks

Prep time: 35 minutes | Cook time: 5 minutes | Serves: 2-4

Ingredients:

2 (8-ounce) boneless ribeye steaks

4 teaspoons Worcestershire sauce

½ teaspoon garlic powder

pepper

4 teaspoons extra virgin olive oil

Salt

Directions:

1. To add flavor to the steaks, apply Worcestershire sauce on both sides and spread it evenly using the back of a spoon. 2. Then, sprinkle garlic powder and coarsely ground black pepper on both sides according to your taste. 3. Drizzle olive oil on both sides and spread it evenly using the back of a spoon. Allow steaks to marinate for 30 minutes. 4. Close the lid and move SmartSwitch to AIRFRY/STOVETOP. Select AIR FRY. set temperature to 390°F, and set time to 5 minutes. Press START/STOP to begin preheating. 5. Place both steaks on the crisper tray, then place the crisper tray in the bottom of the pot. Cook for 5 minutes. 6. Turn steaks over and cook until done. 7. Remove steaks from the pot and let sit 5 minutes. Add salt to taste and serve.

Per Serving: Calories 347; Fat 21.53g; Sodium 351mg; Carbs 6.2g; Fiber 0.3g; Sugar 1.54g; Protein 32.72g

Crispy Calf's Liver

Prep time: 10 minutes | Cook time: 5 minutes | Serves: 4

Ingredients:

1 pound sliced calf's liver

salt and pepper

2 eggs

2 tablespoons milk

½ cup whole wheat flour

1½ cups panko breadcrumbs

½ cup plain breadcrumbs

½ teaspoon salt

¼ teaspoon pepper

Oil for misting or cooking spray

Directions:

1. Slice the liver into strips that are around ½ inch wide, season them with salt and pepper to your liking. 2. Mix egg and milk in a shallow dish, and place wheat flour in another. 3. In a third shallow dish, combine plain breadcrumbs, panko, ½ teaspoon salt, and ¼ teaspoon pepper. 4. Close the lid and move SmartSwitch to AIRFRY/ STOVETOP. Select AIR FRY. set temperature to 390°F, and set time to 5 minutes. Press START/STOP to begin preheating. 5. Dip liver strips in flour, egg wash, and then breadcrumbs, pressing in coating slightly to make crumbs stick. 6. Cooking half the liver at a time, place strips on the crisper tray, close but not touching. 7. Spray them cooking spray. Then place the tray in the bottom of the pot. Cook for 4 to 5 minutes or until done to your preference. 8. Repeat the process for the remaining liver.

Per Serving: Calories 560; Fat 35.72g; Sodium 1941mg; Carbs 31.64g; Fiber 2.8g; Sugar 3.29g; Protein 27.13g

Cheese Sausage Calzones

Prep time: 30 minutes | Cook time: 20 minutes | Serves: 8

Ingredients:

Filling:

¼ pound ground pork sausage

½ teaspoon chile powder

¼ teaspoon ground cumin

⅛ teaspoon garlic powder

⅛ teaspoon onion powder

⅛ teaspoon oregano

½ cup ricotta cheese

1-ounce sharp Cheddar cheese, shredded

2 ounces Pepper Jack cheese, shredded

1 4-ounce can chopped green chiles, drained

Oil for misting or cooking spray

Salsa, sour cream, or guacamole

Crust:

2 cups white wheat flour, plus more for kneading and rolling

1 package (¼ ounce) RapidRise yeast

1 teaspoon salt

½ teaspoon chile powder

½ teaspoon ground cumin

1 cup warm water (115°F to 125°F)

2 teaspoons olive oil

Directions:

1. Close the lid and move SmartSwitch to AIRFRY/STOVETOP. Select BAKE/ROAST, set temperature to 350°F, and set time to 5 minutes. Press START/STOP to begin preheating. 2. Crumble sausage into a baking pan that fits the pot and stir in the filling seasonings: chile powder, cumin, garlic powder, onion powder, and oregano. 3. Place the pan on the crisper tray, then place the crisper tray in the bottom of the pot. Cook for 2 minutes. 4. Stir, breaking apart, and cook for 3 to 4 minutes, until well done. Press START/STOP to stop cooking. 5. Remove and set aside on paper towels to drain. 6. To create the dough, mix flour, yeast, salt, cumin, and chile powder. Then, add warm water and oil until it forms a soft dough. Knead the dough on a lightly floured surface for about 3-4 minutes before letting it rest for 10 minutes. 7. In a separate bowl, combine cooked sausage, chiles, and three cheeses. Finally, cut the dough into 8 pieces. 8. Working with 4 pieces of the dough, press each into a circle about 5 inches in diameter. 9. Top each dough circle with 2 heaping tablespoons of filling. 10. Fold over into a half-moon shape and press edges together. Seal edges firmly to prevent leakage. 11. Spray both sides with oil or cooking spray. Place 4 calzones on the crisper tray, then place the crisper tray in the bottom of the pot. 12. Close the lid and move SmartSwitch to AIRFRY/STOVETOP. Select AIR FRY, set temperature to 360°F, and set time to 5 minutes (unit will need to preheat for 5 minutes, so set an external timer if desired). Press START/STOP to begin cooking. 13. Mist with oil or spray and cook for 2 to 3 minutes, until crust is done and nicely browned. 14. As the initial group of dough is cooking, flatten out the rest of the dough, add the filling and give it the calzone shape. 15. Apply oil or cooking spray on both sides and cook for 5 minutes. If necessary, spray with oil and continue cooking for 2-3 minutes more. 16. You can serve it as it is or with salsa, sour cream, or guacamole.

Per Serving: Calories 341; Fat 16.27g; Sodium 755mg; Carbs 36.24g; Fiber 1.7g; Sugar 0.66g; Protein 12.02g

Air Fried Beef Steaks

Prep time: 10 minutes | Cook time: 15 minutes | Serves: 4

Ingredients:

2 eggs

½ cup buttermilk

1½ cups flour

¾ teaspoon salt

½ teaspoon pepper

1-pound beef cube steaks

Salt and pepper

Oil for misting or cooking spray

Directions:

1. Close the lid and move SmartSwitch to AIRFRY/STOVETOP. Select AIR FRY. set temperature to 360°F, and set time to 5 minutes. Press START/STOP to begin preheating. 2. Whisk eggs and buttermilk in a dish that is not very deep. 3. In another dish that is also not very deep, mix flour, half a teaspoon of salt, and a quarter teaspoon of pepper. 4. Season the cube steaks with salt and pepper according to your preference. 5. Dip the steaks in the flour mixture, then in the egg and buttermilk mixture, and finally in the flour mixture again. 6. Spray oil or cooking spray on both sides of the steaks. 7. Cooking in 2 batches, place steaks on the crisper tray in single layer, then place the tray in the bottom of the pot. Cook for 10 minutes. 8. Spray tops of steaks with oil and cook 5 minutes more or until meat is well done. 9. Repeat to cook remaining steaks.

Per Serving: Calories 414; Fat 11.9g; Sodium 656mg; Carbs 39.41g; Fiber 1.6g; Sugar 3.01g; Protein 34.58g

Barbeque Kielbasa with Pineapple & Peppers

Prep time: 10 minutes | Cook time: 10 minutes | Serves: 2-4

Ingredients:

¾ pound kielbasa sausage

1 cup bell pepper chunks (any color)

1 8-ounce can pineapple chunks in juice, drained

1 tablespoon barbeque seasoning

1 tablespoon soy sauce

Cooking spray

Directions:

1. Close the lid and move SmartSwitch to AIRFRY/STOVETOP. Select AIR FRY. set temperature to 390°F, and set time to 5 minutes. Press START/STOP to begin preheating. 2. Cut sausage into ½-inch slices. 3. In a medium bowl, toss all ingredients together. 4. Spray the crisper tray with nonstick cooking spray. 5. Place sausage mixture on the crisper tray, then place the crisper tray in the bottom of the pot. 6. Cook for about 5 minutes. Stir and cook an additional 5 minutes.

Per Serving: Calories 457; Fat 21.66g; Sodium 1297mg; Carbs 49.05g; Fiber 4.4g; Sugar 35.06g; Protein 22.8g

Greek Lamb Pita Pockets

Prep time: 20 minutes | Cook time: 7 minutes | Serves: 4

Ingredients:

Dressing:

1 cup plain yogurt

1 tablespoon lemon juice

1 teaspoon dried dill weed, crushed

1 teaspoon ground oregano

½ teaspoon salt

Meatballs:

½ pound ground lamb

1 tablespoon diced onion

1 teaspoon dried parsley

1 teaspoon dried dill weed, crushed

¼ teaspoon oregano

¼ teaspoon coriander

¼ teaspoon ground cumin

¼ teaspoon salt

4 pita halves

Suggested Toppings:

Red onion, slivered

Seedless cucumber, thinly sliced

Crumbled feta cheese

Sliced black olives

Chopped fresh peppers

Directions:

1. Mix the ingredients for the dressing and put it in the fridge while you prepare the lamb. 2. In a big bowl, mix all the ingredients for the meatballs except the pita halves and stir well to spread the flavors. 3. Form the mixture into 12 small meatballs, either rounded or slightly flattened, depending on your preference. 4. Close the lid and move SmartSwitch to AIRFRY/STOVETOP. Select AIR FRY. set temperature to 350°F, and set time to 5 minutes. Press START/STOP to begin preheating. 5. Place the meatballs on the crisper tray, then place the crisper tray in the bottom of the pot. Cook for 5 to 7 minutes, until well done. Remove and drain on paper towels. 6. Arrange the meatballs and toppings of your preference in pita pockets and then add a dressing on top before serving.

Per Serving: Calories 342; Fat 17.97g; Sodium 979mg; Carbs 24.56g; Fiber 3g; Sugar 6.61g; Protein 22.47g

Pepperoni Bread Pockets

Prep time: 15 minutes | Cook time: 10 minutes | Serves: 4

Ingredients:

4 bread slices, 1-inch thick

Olive oil for misting

24 slices pepperoni (about 2 ounces)

1 ounce roasted red peppers, drained and patted dry

1-ounce Pepper Jack cheese cut into 4 slices

pizza sauce (optional)

Directions:

1. Close the lid and move SmartSwitch to AIRFRY/STOVETOP. Select AIR FRY. set temperature to 360°F, and set time to 5 minutes. Press START/STOP to begin preheating. 2. Spray both sides of bread slices with olive oil. 3. Stand slices upright and cut a deep slit in the top to create a pocket—almost to the bottom crust but not all the way through. 4. Stuff each bread pocket with 6 slices of pepperoni, a large strip of roasted red pepper, and a slice of cheese. 5. Place bread pockets on the crisper tray, then place the crisper tray in the bottom of the pot. Cook for 8 to 10 minutes, until filling is heated through and bread is lightly browned. 6. Serve with pizza sauce for dipping if desired.

Per Serving: Calories 145; Fat 8.3g; Sodium 372mg; Carbs 10.47g; Fiber 0.6g; Sugar 1.46g; Protein 6.31g

Pork, Beef & Cabbage Egg Rolls

Prep time: 15 minutes | Cook time: 15 minutes | Serves: 8

Ingredients:

¼ pound very lean ground beef

¼ pound lean ground pork

1 tablespoon soy sauce

1 teaspoon olive oil

½ cup grated carrots

2 green onions, chopped

2 cups grated Napa cabbage

¼ cup chopped water chestnuts

¼ teaspoon salt

¼ teaspoon garlic powder

¼ teaspoon black pepper

1 egg

1 tablespoon water

8 egg roll wraps

Oil for misting or cooking spray

Directions:

1. Flip the SmartSwitch to AIRFRY/STOVETOP. Select SEAR/ SAUTÉ, set temperature to 3. Add the beef, pork and soy sauce to the pot, cook until browned, remove cooked meat from the pot, drain, and set aside. 2. Pour off any excess grease from the pot. Add olive oil, carrots, and onions. Sauté until barely tender, about 1 minute. 3. Stir in cabbage, cover, and cook for 1 minute or just until cabbage slightly wilts. Remove from heat. Press START/ STOP to stop cooking. 4. In a large bowl, mix together the cooked meats and vegetables, salt, garlic powder, water chestnuts, and pepper. Stir well. If needed, add more salt to taste. 5. Beat together egg and water in a small bowl. 6. Fill egg roll wrappers, using about ¼ cup of filling for each wrap. Roll up and brush all over with egg wash to seal. Spray very lightly with olive oil or cooking spray. 7. Place 4 egg rolls on the crisper tray, then place the crisper tray in the bottom of the pot. Close the lid and move SmartSwitch to AIRFRY/STOVETOP. Select AIR FRY, set temperature to 390°F, and set time to 4 minutes. Press START/STOP to begin cooking. 8. Turn them over and cook for 3 to 4 more minutes, until golden brown and crispy. 9. Repeat the process for the remaining egg rolls.

Per Serving: Calories 194; Fat 6.69g; Sodium 342mg; Carbs 21.27g; Fiber 1.9g; Sugar 2.99g; Protein 11.91g

Lemon-Rosemary Lamb Chops

Prep time: 15 minutes | Cook time: 22 minutes | Serves: 2-3

Ingredients:

2 teaspoons oil

½ teaspoon ground rosemary

½ teaspoon lemon juice

1-pound lamb chops, approximately 1-inch thick

Salt and pepper

Cooking spray

Directions:

1. Combine the oil, rosemary, and lemon juice, and apply it to all sides of the lamb chops. Add salt and pepper according to your taste. 2. For optimal taste, cover the lamb chops and let them rest in the refrigerator for 15 to 20 minutes. 3. Close the lid and move SmartSwitch to AIRFRY/STOVETOP. Select AIR FRY. set temperature to 360°F, and set time to 5 minutes. Press START/STOP to begin preheating. 4. Spray the crisper tray with nonstick spray and place lamb chops on it, then place the tray in the bottom of the pot. 5. Cook for about 20 minutes. The meat will be juicy but have no remaining pink. 6. Cook for one minute or two longer for well-done chops. For rare chops, stop cooking after about 12 minutes and check for doneness.

Per Serving: Calories 753; Fat 64.98g; Sodium 214mg; Carbs 2.36g; Fiber 0.5g; Sugar 1.63g; Protein 37.36g

Tasty Pizza Tortilla Rolls

Prep time: 15 minutes | Cook time: 15 minutes | Serves: 4

Ingredients:

1 teaspoon butter

½ medium onion, slivered

½ red or green bell pepper, julienned

4 ounces fresh white mushrooms, chopped

8 flour tortillas (6- or 7-inch size)

½ cup pizza sauce

8 thin slices deli ham

24 pepperoni slices (about 1½ ounces)

1 cup shredded mozzarella cheese (about 4 ounces)

Oil for misting or cooking spray

Directions:

1. Close the lid and move SmartSwitch to AIRFRY/STOVETOP. Select AIR FRY. set temperature to 390°F, and set time to 5 minutes. Press START/STOP to begin preheating. 2. Place butter, onions, bell pepper, and mushrooms in a baking pan that can fit the pot. Place the pan on the crisper tray, then place the crisper tray in the bottom of the pot. Cook for 3 minutes. 3. Stir and cook for additional 3 to 4 minutes until just crisp and tender. Remove pan and set aside. 4. To assemble rolls, spread about 2 teaspoons of pizza sauce on one half of each tortilla. Top with a slice of ham and 3 slices of pepperoni. 5. Divide sautéed vegetables among tortillas and top with cheese. 6. Roll up tortillas, secure with toothpicks if needed, and spray with oil. 7. Place 4 rolls on the crisper tray and cook for 4 minutes. Flip and cook for 3 to 4 minutes, until heated through and lightly browned. 8. Repeat the process for the remaining pizza rolls.

Per Serving: Calories 508; Fat 17.09g; Sodium 1846mg; Carbs 57.3g; Fiber 5.2g; Sugar 6.28g; Protein 30.03g

Air Fried Pork Chops

Prep time: 10 minutes | Cook time: 20 minutes | Serves: 2

Ingredients:

2 bone-in, center cut pork chops, 1-inch thick (10 ounces each)

2 teaspoons Worcestershire sauce

Salt and pepper

Cooking spray

Directions:

1. Move the SmartSwitch to AIRFRY/STOVETOP. Select AIR FRY. set temperature to 360°F, and set time to 5 minutes. Press START/STOP to begin preheating. 2. Rub the Worcestershire sauce into both sides of pork chops. 3. Season with salt and pepper to taste. 4. Spray the crisper tray with cooking spray and place the chops on the crisper tray, side by side. Then place the tray in the bottom of the pot. 5. Cook for 16 to 20 minutes or until well done. Let rest for 5 minutes before serving.

Per Serving: Calories 142; Fat 3.36g; Sodium 545mg; Carbs 3.35g; Fiber 0.4g; Sugar 2.18g; Protein 23.57g

Mini Meat Loaves

Prep time: 15 minutes | Cook time: 18 minutes | Serves: 4

Ingredients:

Sauce:

¼ cup white vinegar

¼ cup brown sugar

2 tablespoons Worcestershire sauce

½ cup ketchup

Meat Loaves:

1 pound very lean ground beef

⅔ cup dry bread (approx. 1 slice torn into small pieces)

1 egg

⅓ cup minced onion

1 teaspoon salt

2 tablespoons ketchup

Directions:

1. Combine all the ingredients for the sauce in a small saucepan and heat until it boils. Take the saucepan off the heat and stir until the brown sugar has fully dissolved. 2. Close the lid and move SmartSwitch to AIRFRY/STOVETOP. Select AIR FRY. set temperature to 360°F, and set time to 5 minutes. Press START/STOP to begin preheating. 3. Mix together the beef, bread, egg, onion, salt, and ketchup in a large bowl. 4. Separate the meat mixture into 4 equal parts and form each one into a thick, circular-shaped patty. Patties will be about 3 to 3½ inches in diameter, and all four should fit easily into the crisper tray at once. 5. Place the patties on the crisper tray, then place the crisper tray in the bottom of the pot. 6. Cook for 16 to 18 minutes, until meat is well done. Baste tops of mini loaves with a small amount of sauce, and cook 1 minute. 7. Serve hot with additional sauce on the side.

Per Serving: Calories 451; Fat 16g; Sodium 1246mg; Carbs 40g; Fiber 1.1g; Sugar 24.13g; Protein 35.37g

Meatball Subs with Marinara Sauce

Prep time: 15 minutes | Cook time: 15 minutes | Serves: 6

Ingredients:

Marinara Sauce:

1 15-ounce can diced tomatoes

1 teaspoon garlic powder

1 teaspoon dried basil

½ teaspoon oregano

⅛ teaspoon salt

1 tablespoon robust olive oil

Meatballs:

¼ pound ground turkey

¾ pound very lean ground beef

1 tablespoon milk

½ cup corn bread pieces

1 egg

¼ teaspoon salt

½ teaspoon dried onion

1 teaspoon garlic powder

¼ teaspoon smoked paprika

¼ teaspoon crushed red pepper

1½ teaspoons dried parsley

¼ teaspoon oregano

2 teaspoons Worcestershire sauce

Sandwiches:

4 large whole-grain sub or hoagie rolls, split

Toppings(sliced or chopped):

Mushrooms

Jalapeño or banana peppers

Red or green bell pepper

Red onions

Grated cheese

Directions:

1. First, put all the ingredients for the marinara sauce in a saucepan and bring them to a boil. Then, reduce the heat and let it simmer for 10 minutes without covering the pan. 2. Next, combine all the ingredients for the meatballs in a large bowl and mix them together, making sure not to overwork the mixture. Overworking it can make the meatballs tough. 3. Finally, divide the meat mixture into 16 equal portions and shape each portion into a ball. 4. Close the lid and move SmartSwitch to AIRFRY/STOVETOP. Select AIR FRY. set temperature to 360°F, and set time to 5 minutes. Press START/STOP to begin preheating. 5. Place the meatballs on the crisper tray, then place the crisper tray in the bottom of the pot. Cook until meat is done and juices run clear, about 9 to 11 minutes. 6. As the meatballs are being cooked, taste the marinara sauce. If you think it needs more seasoning to make it stronger, add some and let it simmer for 5 more minutes. 7. After the meatballs are done, put them on paper towels to remove any excess oil. 8. To make the subs, put four meatballs on each roll, pour some sauce over them, and add your favorite toppings. 9. Serve with extra marinara sauce on the side for dipping.

Per Serving: Calories 325; Fat 13.71g; Sodium 516mg; Carbs 24.83g; Fiber 3.2g; Sugar 7.18g; Protein 25.43g

Delicious Beef Pies

Prep time: 15 minutes | Cook time: 18 minutes | Serves: 8

Ingredients:

Filling:

½ pound lean ground beef

¼ cup finely chopped onion

¼ cup finely chopped green bell pepper

⅛ teaspoon salt

½ teaspoon garlic powder

½ teaspoon red pepper flakes

1 tablespoon low sodium Worcestershire sauce

Crust:

2 cups self-rising flour

¼ cup butter, finely diced

1 cup milk

Egg Wash

1 egg

1 tablespoon water or milk

Oil for misting or cooking spray

Directions:

1. Close the lid and move SmartSwitch to AIRFRY/STOVETOP. Select AIR FRY. set temperature to 390°F, and set time to 5 minutes. Press START/STOP to begin preheating. 2. Mix all filling ingredients well and shape into 4 small patties. 3. Place the patties on the crisper tray, then place the crisper tray in the bottom of the pot. 4. Cook for 10 to 12 minutes or until well done. 5. Place the patties in a large bowl and use a fork and knife to crumble the meat into very small pieces. Then, set it aside. 6. To make the crust, you need to use a pastry blender or fork to mix the butter and flour well. After that, add milk and stir until the dough stiffens. 7. Divide the dough into 8 equal parts and roll each portion into a thin circle on a lightly floured surface, approximately 5 inches in diameter. 8. Place 2 tablespoons of meat filling onto each circle of dough. Use an egg wash to brush around the edge of the dough circle, about ½-inch deep. 9. Fold each circle in half and press the dough's edges all the way around with the tines of a dinner fork to seal it. 10. Finally, brush the tops of the sealed meat pies with the egg wash. Place filled pies in a single layer on the crisper tray. Air fry at 360°F for 4 minutes. Spray tops with oil or cooking spray, turn pies over, and spray bottoms with oil or cooking spray. Cook for an additional 2 minutes. 11. Repeat the process for the remaining pies.

Per Serving: Calories 279; Fat 12.75g; Sodium 515mg; Carbs 26.05g; Fiber 1g; Sugar 2.35g; Protein 14.14g

Crispy Pork Cutlets with Aloha Salsa

Prep time: 15 minutes | Cook time: 10 minutes | Serves: 4

Ingredients:

2 eggs

2 tablespoons milk

¼ cup flour

¼ cup panko breadcrumbs

4 teaspoons sesame seeds

1 pound boneless, thin pork cutlets (⅜- to ½-inch thick)

lemon pepper and salt

¼ cup cornstarch

Oil for misting or cooking spray

Aloha Salsa:

1 cup fresh pineapple, chopped in small pieces

¼ cup red onion, finely chopped

¼ cup green or red bell pepper, chopped

½ teaspoon ground cinnamon

1 teaspoon low-sodium soy sauce

⅛ teaspoon crushed red pepper

⅛ teaspoon ground black pepper

Directions:

1. In a medium bowl, mix together all ingredients for salsa. Cover and refrigerate while cooking pork. 2. Flip the SmartSwitch to AIRFRY/STOVETOP. Select AIR FRY. set temperature to 390°F, and set time to 5 minutes. Press START/STOP to begin preheating. 3. Beat together eggs and milk in shallow dish. 4. Mix flour, panko, and sesame seeds in a separate dish. Season the pork cutlets with lemon pepper and salt. 5. Keep in mind that lemon pepper seasoning already contains salt, so add salt sparingly. 6. Coat the pork cutlets in cornstarch, dip them in egg mixture, and cover them with panko coating. 7. Spray oil or cooking spray on both sides of the pork cutlets. Cook cutlets for 3 minutes. 8. Turn cutlets over, spraying both sides, and continue cooking for 4 to 6 minutes or until well done. 9. Serve fried cutlets with salsa on the side.

Per Serving: Calories 398; Fat 13.5g; Sodium 457mg; Carbs 51.74g; Fiber 3.6g; Sugar 17.35g; Protein 17.54g

Cheese Sausage Calzone

Prep time: 20 minutes | Cook time: 25 minutes | Serves: 8

Ingredients:

Crust:

2 cups white wheat flour, plus more for kneading and rolling

1 package (¼ ounce) RapidRise yeast

1 teaspoon salt

½ teaspoon dried basil

1 cup warm water (115°F to 125°F)

2 teaspoons olive oil

Filling:

¼ pound Italian sausage

½ cup ricotta cheese

4 ounces mozzarella cheese, shredded

¼ cup grated Parmesan cheese

Oil for misting or cooking spray

Marinara sauce for serving

Directions:

1. Flip the SmartSwitch to AIRFRY/STOVETOP. Select AIR FRY. set temperature to 390°F, and set time to 5 minutes. Press START/STOP to begin preheating. 2. Crumble Italian sausage into a baking pan that can fit the pot. Place the pan on the crisper tray, then place the crisper tray in the bottom of the pot. Cook for 5 minutes. 3. Stir, breaking apart, and cook for 3 to 4 minutes, until well done. Press START/STOP to stop cooking. Remove and set aside on paper towels to drain. 4. To make dough, combine flour, yeast, salt, and basil. Add warm water and oil and stir until a soft dough forms. Turn out onto lightly floured board and knead for 3 or 4 minutes. Let dough rest for 10 minutes. 5. To make filling, combine the three cheeses in a medium bowl and mix well. Stir in the cooked sausage. Cut dough into 8 pieces. 6. Working with 4 pieces of the dough, press each into a circle about 5 inches in diameter. Top each dough circle with 2 heaping tablespoons of filling. Fold over to create a half-moon shape and press edges firmly together. Be sure that edges are firmly sealed to prevent leakage. Spray both sides with oil or cooking spray. 7. Place 4 calzones on the crisper tray and place the tray in the bottom of the pot. Close the lid and move SmartSwitch to AIRFRY/STOVETOP. Select AIR FRY, set temperature to 360°F, and set time to 5 minutes. Press START/STOP to begin cooking. Mist with oil and cook for 2 to 3 minutes, until crust is done and nicely browned. 8. While the first batch is cooking, press out the remaining dough, fill, and shape into calzones. 9. Spray both sides with oil and cook for 5 minutes. If needed, mist with oil and continue cooking for 2 to 3 minutes longer. 10. This second batch will cook a little faster than the first because your air fryer is already hot. 11. Serve with marinara sauce on the side for dipping.

Per Serving: Calories 485; Fat 18.07g; Sodium 1323mg; Carbs 53.54g; Fiber 2.9g; Sugar 2.52g; Protein 25.6g

Delicious Steak Fingers

Prep time: 15 minutes | Cook time: 10 minutes | Serves: 4

Ingredients:

4 small beef cube steaks

Salt and pepper

½ cup flour

Oil for misting

Directions:

1. Close the lid and move SmartSwitch to AIRFRY/STOVETOP. Select AIR FRY. set temperature to 390°F, and set time to 5 minutes. Press START/STOP to begin preheating. 2. Slice cube steaks into strips that are 1 inch-wide, then add a little bit of salt and pepper according to your taste. After that, cover all sides of the strips by rolling them in flour. 3. Spray the crisper tray with oil. Place steak strips on the crisper tray in single layer, very close together but not touching. 4. Spray top of steak strips with oil. Then place the tray in the bottom of the pot. 5. Cook for 4 minutes, turn the beef strips over, and spray with oil. 6. After cooking for 4 minutes, use a fork to check if the steak fingers are cooked properly. They should be crispy on the outside with no red juices inside. 7. If necessary, cook for an additional 2 to 4 minutes until they are well done. 8. Repeat the process for the remaining strips.

Per Serving: Calories 390; Fat 13.28g; Sodium 179mg; Carbs 13.04g; Fiber 0.6g; Sugar 0.84g; Protein 51.01g

Air Fried Venison Backstrap

Prep time: 15 minutes | Cook time: 12 minutes | Serves: 4

Ingredients:

2 eggs

¼ cup milk

1 cup whole wheat flour

½ teaspoon salt

¼ teaspoon pepper

1-pound venison backstrap, sliced

Salt and pepper

Oil for misting or cooking spray

Directions:

1. First, whisk eggs and milk in a dish that is not deep. 2. Then, mix flour, salt, and pepper in another shallow dish, and stir them together. Season venison steaks with salt and pepper according to your preference. 3. Coat them in flour, egg mixture, and flour again, ensuring that the coating sticks well. 4. Spray both sides of the steaks with oil or cooking spray. Flip the SmartSwitch to AIRFRY/STOVETOP. Select AIR FRY. set temperature to 360°F, and set time to 5 minutes. Press START/STOP to begin preheating. 5. Cooking in 2 batches, place steaks on the crisper tray in a single layer, then place the tray in the bottom of the pot. Cook for 8 minutes. 6. Spray with oil, turn over, and spray other side. Cook for 2 to 4 minutes longer, until coating is crispy brown and meat is done to your liking. 7. Repeat the process to cook remaining venison.

Per Serving: Calories 353; Fat 9.13g; Sodium 932mg; Carbs 24.23g; Fiber 3.5g; Sugar 2.16g; Protein 42.94g

Meat & Brown Rice Stuffed Bell Peppers

Prep time: 15 minutes | Cook time: 20 minutes | Serves: 4

Ingredients:

¼ pound lean ground pork

¾ pound lean ground beef

¼ cup onion, minced

1 15-ounce can Red Gold crushed tomatoes

1 teaspoon Worcestershire sauce

1 teaspoon barbeque seasoning

1 teaspoon honey

½ teaspoon dried basil

½ cup cooked brown rice

½ teaspoon garlic powder

½ teaspoon oregano

½ teaspoon salt

2 small bell peppers

Directions:

1. Flip the SmartSwitch to AIRFRY/STOVETOP. Select AIR FRY. set temperature to 360°F, and set time to 5 minutes. Press START/STOP to begin preheating. 2. Place pork, beef, and onion in a baking pan that can fit the pot. Place the pan on the crisper tray, then place the crisper tray in the bottom of the pot. Cook for 5 minutes. 3. Stir to break apart chunks and cook 3 more minutes. Continue cooking and stirring in 2-minute intervals until meat is well done. Remove from pan and drain. 4. In a small saucepan, mix together the tomatoes, Worcestershire, honey, barbeque seasoning, and basil. 5. Mix together the cooked meat mixture, rice, oregano, garlic powder, and salt in a large bowl. Add ¼ cup of the seasoned crushed tomatoes. Stir to mix well. 6. Cut peppers in half and remove stems and seeds. 7. Stuff each pepper half with one fourth of the meat mixture. 8. Place the peppers on the crisper tray in the pot and air fry for 10 to 12 minutes, until peppers are crisp tender. 9. Heat remaining tomato sauce. Serve peppers with warm sauce spooned over top.

Per Serving: Calories 283; Fat 11.11g; Sodium 553mg; Carbs 14.87g; Fiber 3.1g; Sugar 5.94g; Protein30.7 g

Flavorful Sloppy Joes

Prep time: 15 minutes | Cook time: 20 minutes | Serves: 4

Ingredients:

Oil for misting or cooking spray

1 pound very lean ground beef

1 teaspoon onion powder

⅓ cup ketchup

¼ cup water

½ teaspoon celery seed

1 tablespoon lemon juice

1½ teaspoons brown sugar

1¼ teaspoons low-sodium Worcestershire sauce

½ teaspoon salt (optional)

½ teaspoon vinegar

⅛ teaspoon dry mustard

Hamburger or slider buns

Directions:

1. Flip the SmartSwitch to AIRFRY/STOVETOP. Select AIR FRY. set temperature to 390°F, and set time to 5 minutes. Press START/STOP to begin preheating. 2. Spray the crisper tray with nonstick cooking spray or olive oil. 3. Break raw ground beef into small chunks and place on the crisper tray. 4. Cook for 5 minutes. Stir to break apart and cook 3 minutes. Stir and cook 2 to 4 minutes longer or until meat is well done. 5. Take out the meat from the pot, strain it, and break it into small pieces using a knife and fork. Clean the crisper tray by rinsing it to remove any remaining meat particles. 6. Combine all the other ingredients, except for the buns, in a baking pan that can fit the pot and mix them thoroughly. 7. Add meat and stir well. Place the pan on the crisper tray, then place the crisper tray in the bottom of the pot. 8. Air fry at 330°F for 5 minutes. Stir and cook for 2 minutes. 9. Scoop onto buns and serve.

Per Serving: Calories 361; Fat 16.68g; Sodium 686mg; Carbs 16.92g; Fiber 0.8g; Sugar 7.98g; Protein 34.83g

Juicy Pork Loin Roast

Prep time: 15 minutes | Cook time: 50 minutes | Serves: 8

Ingredients:

1 tablespoon lime juice

1 tablespoon orange marmalade

1 teaspoon coarse brown mustard

1 teaspoon curry powder

1 teaspoon dried lemongrass

2-pound boneless pork loin roast

Salt and pepper

Cooking spray

Directions:

1. Flip the SmartSwitch to AIRFRY/STOVETOP. Select AIR FRY. set temperature to 360°F, and set time to 5 minutes. Press START/STOP to begin preheating. 2. In a bowl, combine the lime juice, marmalade, curry powder, mustard, and lemongrass, mix well. 3. Apply the mixture evenly on the surface of the pork loin and add salt and pepper to taste. 4. Spray the crisper tray with nonstick spray and place pork roast diagonally on it. Then place the tray in the bottom of the pot. 5. Cook for about 45 to 50 minutes, until roast registers 130°F on a meat thermometer. 6. Wrap roast in foil and let rest for 10 minutes before slicing.

Per Serving: Calories 155; Fat 4.69g; Sodium 85mg; Carbs 1.17g; Fiber 0.3g; Sugar 0.63g; Protein 25.56g

Italian Sausage, Mushrooms & Peppers

Prep time: 10 minutes | Cook time: 25 minutes | Serves: 6

Ingredients:

1 6-ounce can tomato paste

⅔ cup water

1 teaspoon dried parsley flakes

½ teaspoon garlic powder

⅛ teaspoon oregano

½ pound mild Italian bulk sausage

1 tablespoon extra-virgin olive oil

½ large onion, cut in 1-inch chunks

4 ounces fresh mushrooms, sliced

1 large green bell pepper, cut in 1-inch chunks

8 ounces spaghetti, cooked

Parmesan cheese for serving

Directions:

1. In a large saucepan, stir together the tomato paste, tomato sauce, parsley, garlic, water, and oregano. Heat on stovetop over very low heat while preparing the meat and vegetables. 2. Break sausage into small chunks, about ½-inch pieces. Place in a baking pan that can fit the pot of your Ninja Speedi Rapid Cooker & Air Fryer. 3. Flip the SmartSwitch to AIRFRY/STOVETOP. Select AIR FRY. set temperature to 390°F, and set time to 5 minutes. Press START/STOP to begin preheating. 4. Place the pan on the crisper tray, then place the crisper tray in the bottom of the pot. 5. Cook the sausage for 5 minutes, then stir it and cook it for another 5 to 7 minutes until it's well done. 6. Remove the sausage from the pan and drain it on paper towels, then add it to the sauce mixture. If there is any grease left in the pan, remove it with paper towels or pour it off carefully. 7. Next, place onions, mushrooms, and olive oil in the pan and cook for 5 minutes until they are tender. 8. Transfer the cooked onions and mushrooms to the sausage and sauce mixture using a slotted spoon. 9. Then, put the bell pepper chunks in the pan and cook for 6 to 8 minutes until they are tender. 10. Finally, stir the cooked bell pepper into the sausage and sauce mixture and serve it over cooked spaghetti with plenty of Parmesan cheese.

Per Serving: Calories 241; Fat 8.42g; Sodium 378mg; Carbs 35.45g; Fiber 6.5g; Sugar 5.09g; Protein 12.4g

Chapter 5 Fish and Seafood Recipes

Salmon Patties

Prep time: 15 minutes | Cook time: 7 minutes | Serves: 4

Ingredients:

1 tbsp. olive oil

1 tbsp. ghee

¼ tsp. salt

⅛ tsp. pepper `

1 egg

1 cup. almond flour

1 can wild Alaskan pink salmon

Directions:

1. Flip the SmartSwitch to AIRFRY/STOVETOP. Select AIR FRY. set temperature to 380°F, and set time to 5 minutes. Press START/STOP to begin preheating. 2. Drain can of salmon into a bowl and keep liquid. Discard skin and bones and add salt, pepper, and an egg to the salmon. Mix the ingredients together with your hands and form patties. 3. Coat the patties with flour and the remaining egg. 4. If the mixture seems too dry, add some of the reserved liquid from the can of salmon onto the patties. 5. Place the patties on the crisper tray, then place the crisper tray in the bottom of the pot. Cook for 7 minutes till golden, making sure to flip once during cooking process.

Per Serving: Calories 249; Fat 16.29g; Sodium 645mg; Carbs 0.46g; Fiber 0.1g; Sugar 0.25g; Protein 23.87g

Fried Baby Squid

Prep time: 15 minutes | Cook time: 15 minutes | Serves: 6

Ingredients:

½ tsp. salt

½ tsp. Old Bay seasoning

⅓ cup plain cornmeal

½ cup semolina flour

½ cup almond flour

5-6 teaspoons olive oil

1½ pounds baby squid

Directions:

1. Flip the SmartSwitch to AIRFRY/STOVETOP. Select AIR FRY. set temperature to 345°F, and set time to 5 minutes. Press START/STOP to begin preheating. 2. Rinse squid in cold water and slice tentacles, keeping just ¼-inch of the hood in one piece. 3. In a bowl, mix together 1-2 pinches of pepper, salt, cornmeal, Old Bay seasoning, and both flours. 4. Dredge squid pieces into flour mixture and place on the crisper tray, then place the crisper tray in the bottom of the pot. Spray liberally with olive oil. 5. Cook for 15 minutes till coating turns a golden brown.

Per Serving: Calories 214; Fat 6.13g; Sodium 328mg; Carbs 18.41g; Fiber 1g; Sugar 0g; Protein 20.01g

Crispy Panko-Crusted Tilapia

Prep time: 15 minutes | Cook time: 11 minutes | Serves: 3

Ingredients:

2 tsp. Italian seasoning

2 tsp. lemon pepper

⅓ cup panko breadcrumbs

⅓ cup egg whites

⅓ cup almond flour

3 tilapia fillets

Olive oil

Directions:

1. Flip the SmartSwitch to AIRFRY/STOVETOP. Select AIR FRY. set temperature to 400°F, and set time to 5 minutes. Press START/STOP to begin preheating. 2. Separate panko, egg whites, and flour into individual bowls. Combine lemon pepper and Italian seasoning with breadcrumbs. 3. Dry the tilapia fillets with a pat and coat them in flour, then egg, and finally in the breadcrumb mixture. 4. Place the tilapia fillets on the crisper tray, then place the crisper tray in the bottom of the pot. Spray lightly with olive oil. 5. Cook for 10-11 minutes, ensuring to flip halfway through the cooking time.

Per Serving: Calories 154; Fat 2.27g; Sodium 263mg; Carbs 6.07g; Fiber 0.8g; Sugar 2.15g; Protein 27.26g

Salmon-Carrot Croquettes

Prep time: 15 minutes | Cook time: 10 minutes | Serves: 6

Ingredients:

Panko breadcrumbs

Almond flour

2 egg whites

2 tbsp. chopped chives

2 tbsp. minced garlic cloves

½ cup chopped onion

⅔ cup grated carrots

1 pound chopped salmon fillet

Directions:

1. Close the lid and move SmartSwitch to AIRFRY/STOVETOP. Select AIR FRY. set temperature to 350°F, and set time to 5 minutes. Press START/STOP to begin preheating. 2. Mix together all ingredients except breadcrumbs, flour, and egg whites. 3. Shape mixture into balls. Then coat them in flour, then egg, and then breadcrumbs. Drizzle with olive oil. 4. Place coated salmon balls on the crisper tray, then place the crisper tray in the bottom of the pot. Cook for 6 minutes. 5. Stir and cook for 4 more minutes until golden.

Per Serving: Calories 156; Fat 5.85g; Sodium 392mg; Carbs 6.88g; Fiber 0.8g; Sugar 1.55g; Protein 17.93g

Spicy Cod Tacos

Prep time: 15 minutes | Cook time: 15 minutes | Serves: 4

Ingredients:

1-pound cod

1 tbsp. cumin

½ tbsp. chili powder

1½ cup almond flour

1½ cup coconut flour

10 ounces Mexican beer

2 eggs

Lettuce

Directions:

1. Close the lid and move SmartSwitch to AIRFRY/STOVETOP. Select AIR FRY. set temperature to 375°F, and set time to 5 minutes. Press START/STOP to begin preheating. 2. Beat the eggs and beer until combined in a bowl. Mix the flours, cumin, pepper, salt, and chili powder together in a separate bowl. 3. Cut the cod into big pieces and dip them first into the egg mixture, then into the flour mixture. 4. Spray the crisper tray with olive oil and place the coated codpieces on it, then place the tray in the bottom of the pot. 5. Cook for 15 minutes. Serve on lettuce leaves topped with homemade salsa!

Per Serving: Calories 192; Fat 6.17g; Sodium 523mg; Carbs 6.03g; Fiber 1.6g; Sugar 2.8g; Protein 23.12g

Bacon Wrapped Sea Scallops

Prep time: 15 minutes | Cook time: 6 minutes | Serves: 4

Ingredients:

1 tsp. paprika

1 tsp. lemon pepper

5 slices of center-cut bacon

20 raw sea scallops

Directions:

1. First, rinse and drain the scallops and then put them on paper towels to remove any extra moisture. Cut the bacon into small pieces and wrap each scallop with one piece of bacon, securing it with toothpicks. Finally, sprinkle the wrapped scallops with paprika and lemon pepper seasoning. 2. Flip the SmartSwitch to AIRFRY/ STOVETOP. Select AIR FRY. set temperature to 400°F, and set time to 5 minutes. Press START/STOP to begin preheating. 3. Spray the crisper tray with olive oil and add scallops, then place the tray in the bottom of the pot. 4. Cook for 5-6 minutes, making sure to flip halfway through.

Per Serving: Calories 190; Fat 13.23g; Sodium 448mg; Carbs 4.03g; Fiber 0.4g; Sugar 0.9g; Protein 13.42g

Garlicky Parmesan Shrimp

Prep time: 15 minutes | Cook time: 10 minutes | Serves: 6

Ingredients:

2 tbsp. olive oil

1 tsp. onion powder

1 tsp. basil

½ tsp. oregano

1 tsp. pepper

⅔ cup grated parmesan cheese

4 minced garlic cloves

2 pounds of jumbo cooked shrimp (peeled/deveined)

Directions:

1. Close the lid and move SmartSwitch to AIRFRY/STOVETOP. Select AIR FRY. set temperature to 350°F, and set time to 5 minutes. Press START/STOP to begin preheating. 2. Mix all seasonings together and gently toss shrimp with mixture until well coated. 3. Spray the crisper tray with olive oil and add seasoned shrimp, then place the tray in the bottom of the pot. 4. Cook for 8-10 minutes. Squeeze lemon juice over shrimp right before serving!

Per Serving: Calories 246; Fat 9.7g; Sodium 1518mg; Carbs 3.32g; Fiber 0.3g; Sugar 0.44g; Protein 34.4g

Delicious Honey Glazed Salmon

Prep time: 10 minutes | Cook time: 13 minutes | Serves: 2

Ingredients:

1 tsp. water

3 tsp. rice wine vinegar

6 tbsp. low-sodium soy sauce

6 tbsp. raw honey

2 salmon fillets

Directions:

1. Mix water, honey, vinegar, and soy sauce, and then pour half of the mixture into a bowl. Submerge the salmon in the marinade and refrigerate for 2 hours. 2. Close the lid and move SmartSwitch to AIRFRY/STOVETOP. Select AIR FRY. set temperature to 350°F, and set time to 5 minutes. Press START/STOP to begin preheating. 3. Place the salmon on the crisper and place the tray in the bottom of the pot. 4. Cook for 8 minutes, flipping halfway through the cooking time. Baste salmon with some of the remaining marinade mixture and cook another 5 minutes. 5. To create a sauce for salmon, heat the leftover marinade mixture in a saucepan until it starts simmering. Allow it to simmer for two minutes and then pour it over the salmon when serving.

Per Serving: Calories 621; Fat 14.12g; Sodium 1774mg; Carbs 54.31g; Fiber 0.4g; Sugar 51.95g; Protein 69.24g

Crispy Coconut Shrimp

Prep time: 15 minutes | Cook time: 10 minutes | Serves: 4

Ingredients:

1 cup breadcrumbs

1 cup dried coconut, unsweetened

1 cup almond flour

Sea salt to taste

2 lbs. shrimp

1 cup egg whites

Directions:

1. In a medium bowl, mix together the coconut and breadcrumbs. Season lightly with sea salt. In a separate bowl, add flour, and in a third bowl, add egg whites. 2. Close the lid and move SmartSwitch to AIRFRY/STOVETOP. Select AIR FRY. set temperature to 340°F, and set time to 5 minutes. Press START/STOP to begin preheating. 3. Dip each shrimp into flour, egg whites, then the breadcrumbs. 4. Place the shrimp on the crisper tray, then place the crisper tray in the bottom of the pot. Cook for 10 minutes and serve with preferred dipping sauce.

Per Serving: Calories 344; Fat 2.96g; Sodium 699mg; Carbs 22.17g; Fiber 1.9g; Sugar 3.68g; Protein 56.31g

Simple Air-Fried Shrimp

Prep time: 10 minutes | Cook time: 5 minutes | Serves: 4

Ingredients:

1¼ lbs. shrimp, peeled and deveined

¼ teaspoon salt

½ teaspoon paprika

1 tablespoon olive oil

¼ cayenne pepper

½ teaspoon Old Bay seasoning

Directions:

1. Close the lid and move SmartSwitch to AIRFRY/STOVETOP. Select AIR FRY. set temperature to 400°F, and set time to 5 minutes. Press START/STOP to begin preheating. 2. Mix all the ingredients in a bowl. Place the seasoned shrimp on the crisper tray, then place the crisper tray in the bottom of the pot. Cook for 5 minutes. Serve warm.

Per Serving: Calories 174; Fat 5.35g; Sodium 1379mg; Carbs 0.49g; Fiber 0.2g; Sugar 0.18g; Protein 29.05g

Air-Fried Crab Croquettes

Prep time: 15 minutes | Cook time: 18 minutes | Serves: 6

Ingredients:

1 lb. crab meat

1 cup breadcrumbs

2 egg whites

Salt and black pepper to taste

½ teaspoon parsley, chopped

¼ teaspoon chives

¼ teaspoon tarragon

2 tablespoon celeries, chopped

4 tablespoon mayonnaise

4 tablespoons light sour cream

1 teaspoon olive oil

½ teaspoon lime juice

½ cup red pepper, chopped

¼ cup onion, chopped

Directions:

1. Close the lid and move SmartSwitch to AIRFRY/STOVETOP. Select AIR FRY. set temperature to 355°F, and set time to 5 minutes. Press START/STOP to begin preheating. 2. In a bowl, mix together the breadcrumbs, salt and pepper. In a second bowl, add the egg whites. In a separate large bowl, add all the remaining ingredients and mix well. 3. Make croquettes from crab mixture and dip into egg whites, and then into breadcrumbs. 4. Place on the crisper tray, then place the crisper tray in the bottom of the pot. Cook for 18 minutes. Serve warm.

Per Serving: Calories 380; Fat 9.13g; Sodium 242mg; Carbs 44.43g; Fiber 14.6g; Sugar 2.6g; Protein 33.59g

Creamy Salmon

Prep time: 15 minutes | Cook time: 10 minutes | Serves: 2

Ingredients:

¾ lb. salmon, cut into 6 pieces

Salt to taste

¼ cup plain yogurt

1 tablespoon dill, chopped

3 tablespoons light sour cream

1 tablespoon olive oil

Directions:

1. Close the lid and move SmartSwitch to AIRFRY/STOVETOP. Select AIR FRY. set temperature to 285°F, and set time to 5 minutes. Press START/STOP to begin preheating. 2. Season the salmon with salt and place it on the crisper tray, then place the crisper tray in the bottom of the pot. 3. Spray the salmon with olive oil. Air-fry for 10 minutes. Mix the dill, sour cream, yogurt, and some salt. 4. Place salmon on serving dish and drizzle with creamy sauce.

Per Serving: Calories 386; Fat 24.35g; Sodium 879mg; Carbs 3.12g; Fiber 0.2g; Sugar 2.25g; Protein 37.07g

Crispy Cod Sticks

Prep time: 10 minutes | Cook time: 12 minutes | Serves: 5

Ingredients:

2 large eggs, beaten

3 tablespoon milk

2 cups breadcrumbs

1 lb. cod fillets

1 cup almond meal

Salt and pepper to taste

Directions:

1. Close the lid and move SmartSwitch to AIRFRY/STOVETOP. Select AIR FRY. set temperature to 350°F, and set time to 5 minutes. Press START/STOP to begin preheating. 2. Combine egg and milk in a bowl. In a separate shallow dish, mix breadcrumbs with pepper and salt. In another dish, place the almond meal. 3. Take the cod sticks and roll them in the almond meal, then dip them in the egg mixture, and finally coat them with the breadcrumb mixture. 4. Place the coated cod sticks on the crisper tray, then place the crisper tray in the bottom of the pot. 5. Cook for 12 minutes and flip halfway through the cooking time. Serve hot.

Per Serving: Calories 266; Fat 4.9g; Sodium 599mg; Carbs 32.67g; Fiber 2.1g; Sugar 3.64g; Protein 21.21g

Juicy Barbecued Shrimp

Prep time: 15 minutes | Cook time: 15 minutes | Serves: 4

Ingredients:

4 cups of shrimp

1½ cups barbeque sauce

1 fresh lime, cut into quarters

Directions:

1. Close the lid and move SmartSwitch to AIRFRY/STOVETOP. Select AIR FRY. set temperature to 360°F, and set time to 5 minutes. Press START/STOP to begin preheating. 2. Place the shrimp in a bowl with barbeque sauce. Stir gently. Allow shrimps to marinade for at least 5-minutes. 3. Place the shrimp on the crisper tray, then place the crisper tray in the bottom of the pot. Cook for 15 minutes. 4. Remove from the pot and squeeze lime over shrimps.

Per Serving: Calories 159; Fat 1.91g; Sodium 1801mg; Carbs 7.48g; Fiber 1.8g; Sugar 4.03g; Protein 27.69g

Crispy Breaded Shrimp

Prep time: 10 minutes | Cook time: 16 minutes | Serves: 8

Ingredients:

4 egg whites

1 cup almond flour

2 lbs. shrimp, peeled and deveined

½ teaspoon cayenne pepper

2 tablespoons olive oil

1 cup breadcrumbs

Salt and black pepper to taste

Directions:

1. Combine flour, pepper, and salt in a dish. Beat egg whites in a small bowl. Mix breadcrumbs, cayenne pepper, and salt in a separate bowl. 2. Close the lid and move SmartSwitch to AIRFRY/STOVETOP. Select AIR FRY. set temperature to 400°F, and set time to 5 minutes. Press START/STOP to begin preheating. 3. Coat the shrimp with flour mixture, dip in egg white, then finally coat with breadcrumbs. 4. Place shrimp on the crisper tray, and spray with olive oil. 5. Then place the tray in the bottom of the pot and cook in batches for 8-minutes each.

Per Serving: Calories 192; Fat 4.8g; Sodium 262mg; Carbs 10.47g; Fiber 0.7g; Sugar 1.26g; Protein 26.55g

Spicy Cheese Tilapia

Prep time: 10 minutes | Cook time: 10 minutes | Serves: 4

Ingredients:

1 lb. tilapia fillets

1 tablespoon olive oil

Salt and pepper to taste

2 teaspoons paprika

1 tablespoon parsley, chopped

¾ cup parmesan cheese, grated

Directions:

1. Close the lid and move SmartSwitch to AIRFRY/STOVETOP. Select AIR FRY. set temperature to 400°F, and set time to 5 minutes. Press START/STOP to begin preheating. 2. Combine parmesan cheese, paprika, parsley, salt, and pepper. Then sprinkle olive oil on the tilapia fillets and coat them with the mixture of paprika and cheese. 3. Place the coated tilapia fillets on aluminum foil. Place on the crisper tray, then place the crisper tray in the bottom of the pot. Cook for 10 minutes, serve warm.

Per Serving: Calories 226; Fat 10.7g; Sodium 399mg; Carbs 4.35g; Fiber 0.6g; Sugar 0.71g; Protein 28.52g

Cheese Salmon with Parsley

Prep time: 10 minutes | Cook time: 11 minutes | Serves: 5

Ingredients:

2 lbs. salmon fillet

Salt and pepper to taste

½ cup parmesan cheese, grated

¼ cup parsley, fresh, chopped

2 garlic cloves, minced

Directions:

1. Close the lid and move SmartSwitch to AIRFRY/STOVETOP. Select AIR FRY. set temperature to 350°F, and set time to 5 minutes. Press START/STOP to begin preheating. 2. Put the salmon skin side facing down on aluminum foil and cover with another piece of foil. 3. Place on the crisper tray, then place the crisper tray in the bottom of the pot. Cook for 10 minutes. 4. Remove the salmon from foil and top it with minced garlic, parsley, parmesan cheese, and pepper. 5. Return salmon to the air fryer and cook for 1 more minute.

Per Serving: Calories 326; Fat 15.84g; Sodium 969mg; Carbs 2.83g; Fiber 0.3g; Sugar 0.5g; Protein 40.62g

Herbed Salmon Fillets

Prep time: 10 minutes | Cook time: 8 minutes | Serves: 2

Ingredients:

½ lb. salmon fillet

¼ teaspoon thyme

1 teaspoon garlic powder

½ teaspoon cayenne pepper

½ teaspoon paprika

¼ teaspoon sage

¼ teaspoon oregano

Salt and pepper to taste

Directions:

1. Close the lid and move SmartSwitch to AIRFRY/STOVETOP. Select AIR FRY. set temperature to 350°F, and set time to 5 minutes. Press START/STOP to begin preheating. 2. Rub the seasoning all over the salmon. 3. Place the seasoned salmon fillet on the crisper tray, then place the crisper tray in the bottom of the pot. Cook for 8 minutes, serve warm.

Per Serving: Calories 192; Fat 8.36g; Sodium 494mg; Carbs 4.02g; Fiber 0.9g; Sugar 1.3g; Protein 24.27g

Crispy Fish Taco

Prep time: 10 minutes | Cook time: 13 minutes | Serves: 4

Ingredients:

12-ounce cod fillet

Salt and black pepper to taste

1 cup tempura butter

1 cup breadcrumbs

1 lemon, juiced

½ cup guacamole

6-flour tortillas

2 tablespoons cilantro, freshly chopped

½ cup salsa

Directions:

1. Close the lid and move SmartSwitch to AIRFRY/STOVETOP. Select AIR FRY. set temperature to 340°F, and set time to 5 minutes. Press START/STOP to begin preheating. 2. Cut the cod fillets lengthwise into 2-inch pieces and season with salt and pepper. Dip each cod strip into tempura butter then into breadcrumbs. 3. Place the cod fillets on the crisper tray, then place the crisper tray in the bottom of the pot. Cook for 13 minutes. 4. Take a tortilla and apply a layer of guacamole on it. Next, put a piece of cod on top of the tortilla and sprinkle chopped cilantro and salsa over it. 5. Squeeze lemon juice on it and fold it before serving.

Per Serving: Calories 753; Fat 55.06g; Sodium 1147mg; Carbs 45.94g; Fiber 4.6g; Sugar 4.68g; Protein 20.96g

Lemony Salmon & Asparagus

Prep time: 10 minutes | Cook time: 15 minutes | Serves: 4

Ingredients:

4 salmon fillets

4 asparagus

2 tablespoons butter

3 lemons, sliced

Salt and pepper to taste

Directions:

1. Close the lid and move SmartSwitch to AIRFRY/STOVETOP. Select AIR FRY. set temperature to 300°F, and set time to 5 minutes. Press START/STOP to begin preheating. 2. To prepare four servings, grab four sheets of aluminum foil. In a bowl, mix asparagus, lemon juice, pepper, and salt, then divide the mixture evenly among the four sheets. 3. Place a salmon fillet on top of each pile of asparagus and add lemon slices on top of the salmon fillets. 4. Fold foil tightly to seal parcel. Place on the crisper tray, then place the crisper tray in the bottom of the pot. Cook for 15 minutes. Serve warm.

Per Serving: Calories 470; Fat 19.88g; Sodium 286mg; Carbs 4.17g; Fiber 0.6g; Sugar 1.79g; Protein 65.95g

Chapter 6 Snack and Appetizer Recipes

Chipotle Bacon-Jicama Hash

Prep time: 10 minutes | Cook time: 12 minutes | Serves: 2

Ingredients:

4 slices bacon, chopped

12 oz. jicama, peeled and diced

4 oz. purple onion, chopped

1 oz. green bell pepper (or poblano), seeded and chopped

4 tbsp Chipotle mayonnaise

Directions:

1. Add the bacon to the pot. Flip the SmartSwitch to AIRFRY/STOVETOP. Select SEAR/ SAUTÉ, set temperature to Hi5, press START/STOP to begin cooking, cook until browned. 2. Remove and place on a towel to drain the grease. 3. You can utilize the leftover grease to cook the onions and jicama until they turn golden brown. 4. Afterwards, include the bell pepper and cook the mixture until it becomes soft. 5. When it's ready, put the hash onto two plates and serve it with Chipotle mayonnaise.

Per Serving: Calories 397; Fat 30.18g; Sodium 489mg; Carbs 21.98g; Fiber 9.4g; Sugar 7.32g; Protein 10.26g

Sautéed Spinach with Bacon & Shallots

Prep time: 10 minutes | Cook time: 25 minutes | Serves: 4

Ingredients:

16 oz. raw spinach

½ cup chopped white onion

½ cup chopped shallot

½ pound raw bacon slices

2 tbsp butter

Directions:

1. Slice the bacon strips into small narrow pieces. 2. Add butter to the pot. Flip the SmartSwitch to AIRFRY/ STOVETOP. Select SEAR/ SAUTÉ, set temperature to 4, press START/STOP to begin cooking. 3. Once the butter is heated, add the chopped onion, shallots and bacon. 4. Sauté for 15-20 minutes or until the onions start to caramelize and the bacon is cooked. 5. Add the spinach and stir frequently to ensure the leaves touch the pot while cooking. 6. Cover and sauté for around 5 minutes, stir and continue until wilted. Serve!

Per Serving: Calories 340; Fat 29.52g; Sodium 447mg; Carbs 10.1g; Fiber 3.2g; Sugar 1.94g; Protein 10.99g

Homemade Bacon-Wrapped Sausage Skewers

Prep time: 10 minutes | Cook time: 5 minutes | Serves: 2

Ingredients:

5 Italian chicken sausages   10 slices bacon

Directions:

1. Close the lid and move SmartSwitch to AIRFRY/STOVETOP. Select AIR FRY. set temperature to 370°F, and set time to 5 minutes. Press START/STOP to begin preheating. 2. Cut the sausage into four equal parts. Halve the bacon slices. 3. Take each piece of sausage and wrap it with a piece of bacon. Skewer the sausage. 4. Place on the crisper tray, then place the crisper tray in the bottom of the pot. Cook for 4-5 minutes until browned.

Per Serving: Calories 621; Fat 48.81g; Sodium 963mg; Carbs 2.12g; Fiber 0g; Sugar 1.08g; Protein 20.49g

Air Fried Brussels Sprouts & Bacon

Prep time: 10 minutes | Cook time: 25 minutes | Serves: 3

Ingredients:

24 oz. Brussels sprouts   6 strips bacon

¼ cup fish sauce   Pepper to taste

¼ cup bacon grease

Directions:

1. Close the lid and move SmartSwitch to AIRFRY/STOVETOP. Select AIR FRY. set temperature to 360°F, and set time to 5 minutes. Press START/STOP to begin preheating. 2. De-stem and quarter the Brussels sprouts. 3. Mix them with the bacon grease and fish sauce. 4. Slice the bacon into small strips and cook for 2-3 minutes in a skillet over medium heat. 5. Add the bacon and pepper to the sprouts. 6. Spread onto a greased pan and place the pan on the crisper tray, then place the crisper tray in the bottom of the pot. Cook for 25 minutes. 7. Stir every 5 minute or so. Serve.

Per Serving: Calories 291; Fat 20.75g; Sodium 2113mg; Carbs 21.87g; Fiber 8.9g; Sugar 5.86g; Protein 9.96g

Cheese Ham Rolls

Prep time: 10 minutes | Cook time: 5 minutes | Serves: 4

Ingredients:

16 slices ham

16 slices thin Swiss cheese

1 package chive and onion cream cheese (8 oz.)

Directions:

1. Put the ham on a cutting board. 2. Use a paper towel to remove any excess moisture from the ham slices. 3. Spread 2 teaspoons of Swiss cheese thinly over each slice of ham. 4. Place a slice of cheese that's half an inch thick on the clean part of the ham. 5. Fold the ham over the cheese and roll it up so that the cheese is on the inside. 6. Leave it as is, or slice into smaller rolls. 7. Close the lid and move SmartSwitch to AIRFRY/STOVETOP. Select AIR FRY. set temperature to 350°F, and set time to 5 minutes. Press START/STOP to begin preheating. 8. Place the rolls on the crisper tray, then place the crisper tray in the bottom of the pot. Cook for 5 minutes. Serve.

Per Serving: Calories 656; Fat 48.22g; Sodium 1634mg; Carbs 14.75g; Fiber 0g; Sugar 11.94g; Protein 41.89g

Cheesy Broccoli

Prep time: 10 minutes | Cook time: 30 minutes | Serves: 6

Ingredients:

4 cups broccoli florets

¼ cup heavy whipping cream

¼ cup ranch dressing

Kosher salt and pepper to taste

½ cup sharp cheddar cheese, shredded

Directions:

1. Close the lid and move SmartSwitch to AIRFRY/STOVETOP. Select AIR FRY. set temperature to 375°F, and set time to 5 minutes. Press START/STOP to begin preheating. 2. In a bowl, combine all of the ingredients until the broccoli is well-coated. 3. Place the broccoli mixture in a baking dish that can fit the pot. Place the baking dish on the crisper tray, then place the crisper tray in the bottom of the pot. 4. Cook for 30 minutes. 5. Take out of the pot and mix. 6. If the florets are not tender, cook for another 5 minutes until tender. Serve!

Per Serving: Calories 106; Fat 9.63g; Sodium 162mg; Carbs 2.31g; Fiber 0.8g; Sugar 1.12g; Protein 3.49g

Garlicky Parmesan Cauliflower

Prep time: 10 minutes | Cook time: 20 minutes | Serves: 4

Ingredients:

¾ cup cauliflower florets

2 tbsp butter

1 clove garlic, sliced thinly

2 tbsp shredded parmesan

1 pinch of salt

Directions:

1. Close the lid and move SmartSwitch to AIRFRY/STOVETOP. Select BAKE/ROAST, set temperature to 350°F, and set time to 5 minutes. Press START/STOP to begin preheating. 2. Melt the butter with the garlic for 5-10 minutes in a skillet over low heat. 3. Strain the garlic in a sieve. 4. Add the cauliflower, garlic, parmesan and salt to a baking dish that can fit the pot, stir well. Place the baking dish on the crisper tray, then place the crisper tray in the bottom of the pot. 5. Bake for 20 minutes or until golden.

Per Serving: Calories 66; Fat 5.94g; Sodium 197mg; Carbs 2.25g; Fiber 0.4g; Sugar 0.43g; Protein 1.49g

Lemony Sugar Snap Peas

Prep time: 10 minutes | Cook time: 5 minutes | Serves: 4

Ingredients:

3 cups sugar snap peas

½ tbsp lemon juice

2 tbsp bacon fat

2 tsp garlic

½ tsp red pepper flakes

1 tsp lemon zest

Directions:

1. Add the bacon fat to the pot. Flip the SmartSwitch to AIRFRY/STOVETOP. Select SEAR/ SAUTÉ, set temperature to 3, press START/STOP to begin cooking, Add the garlic and cook for 2 minutes. 2. Add the sugar peas and lemon juice and cook for 2-3 minutes. 3. Transfer to a serving plate and sprinkle with red pepper flakes and lemon zest.

Per Serving: Calories 64; Fat 1.68g; Sodium 71mg; Carbs 9.27g; Fiber 3.6g; Sugar 0.38g; Protein 3.72g

Flaxseed Cheese Chips

Prep time: 10 minutes | Cook time: 15 minutes | Serves: 2

Ingredients:

1½ cup cheddar cheese

4 tbsp ground flaxseed meal

Seasonings of your choice

Directions:

1. Close the lid and move SmartSwitch to AIRFRY/STOVETOP. Select BAKE/ROAST, set temperature to 380°F, and set time to 5 minutes. Press START/STOP to begin preheating. 2. Cut cheddar cheese into small chips, onto a non-stick pan that can fit your pot. 3. Spread out a pinch of flax seed on each chip. Add your desired seasonings. Place the pan on the crisper tray, then place the crisper tray in the bottom of the pot. 4. Bake for 10-15 minutes.

Per Serving: Calories 455; Fat 37.35g; Sodium 566mg; Carbs 7.19g; Fiber 5.7g; Sugar 0.58g; Protein 24.15g

Lemon-Garlic Bacon & Swiss Chard

Prep time: 10 minutes | Cook time: 10 minutes | Serves: 2

Ingredients:

4 slices bacon, chopped

2 tbsp butter

2 tbsp fresh lemon juice

½ tsp garlic paste

1 bunch Swiss chard, stems removed, leaves cut into 1-inch pieces

Directions:

1. Add the bacon to the pot. Flip the SmartSwitch to AIRFRY/STOVETOP. Select SEAR/ SAUTÉ, set temperature to 3, press START/STOP to begin cooking. Cook until the bacon begins to brown. 2. Melt the butter in the pot and add the lemon juice and garlic paste. 3. Add the chard leaves and cook until they begin to wilt. 4. Cover and turn up the heat to Hi5. Cook for 3 minutes. 5. Mix well, sprinkle with salt and serve.

Per Serving: Calories 413; Fat 32.98g; Sodium 1401mg; Carbs 20.42g; Fiber 8.1g; Sugar 6.33g; Protein 15.73g

Herbed Cauliflower Hash

Prep time: 10 minutes | Cook time: 30 minutes | Serves: 4

Ingredients:

1 large head of cauliflower divided into florets.

4 large eggs

2 garlic cloves (minced)

1½ tsp herbs (whatever your favorite is - basil, oregano, thyme)

½ tsp salt

Directions:

1. Put parchment paper on a baking pan that can fit the pot. 2. Use a food processor to chop the cauliflower into small pieces resembling rice. 3. Then, transfer the riced cauliflower to a saucepan, add ¼ cup of water, and cook on medium high heat for 10 minutes until it becomes tender. 4. Drain the excess liquid. Dry with a clean kitchen towel. 5. Mix the cauliflower, eggs, garlic, herbs and salt. 6. Make 4 thin circles on the parchment paper. 7. Flip the SmartSwitch to AIRFRY/STOVETOP. Select BAKE/ROAST, set temperature to 375°F, and set time to 5 minutes. Press START/STOP to begin preheating. 8. Place the pan on the crisper tray, then place the crisper tray in the bottom of the pot. 9. Bake for 20 minutes, until dry.

Per Serving: Calories 74; Fat 4.71g; Sodium 319mg; Carbs 4.47g; Fiber 1.4g; Sugar 1.38g; Protein 4.08g

Homemade Mayonnaise

Prep time: 10 minutes | Cook time: 0 minutes | Serves: 4

Ingredients:

1 large egg

Juice from 1 lemon.

1 tsp dry mustard

½ tsp black pepper

1 cup avocado oil

Directions:

1. In a container, mix together the egg and lemon juice and leave for 20 minutes. 2. Then, mix in the dry mustard, pepper, and avocado oil. 3. Next, place an electric whisk into the container and blend for 30 seconds. 4. Finally, transfer the mixture to a sealed container and store it in the refrigerator.

Per Serving: Calories 500; Fat 55.71g; Sodium 16mg; Carbs 1.29g; Fiber 0.2g; Sugar 0.34g; Protein 0.8g

Homemade Hollandaise Sauce

Prep time: 10 minutes | Cook time: 1 minute | Serves: 8

Ingredients:

8 large egg yolks

½ tsp salt

2 tbsp fresh lemon juice

1 cup unsalted butter

Directions:

1. In a blender, blend together the egg yolks, salt, and lemon juice until the mixture becomes smooth. 2. Next, melt the butter in the microwave for approximately 60 seconds until it turns into a liquid and becomes hot. 3. Turn on the blender at a low speed and gradually pour the melted butter into the mixture until the sauce starts to thicken. Finally, serve the sauce.

Per Serving: Calories 260; Fat 26.6g; Sodium 218mg; Carbs 1.16g; Fiber 0g; Sugar 0.26g; Protein 4.84g

Buttery Green Beans and Pine Nuts

Prep time: 10 minutes | Cook time: 10 minutes | Serves: 4

Ingredients:

1 lb. green beans, trimmed

1 cup butter

2 cloves garlic, minced

1 cup toasted pine nuts

Directions:

1. Boil a pan of water. 2. Add the green beans and cook until tender for 5 minutes. 3. Add butter to the pot. Flip the SmartSwitch to AIRFRY/STOVETOP. Select SEAR/ SAUTÉ, set temperature to 4, press START/STOP to begin cooking. Add the garlic and pine nuts and sauté for 2 minutes or until the pine nuts are lightly browned. 4. Transfer the green beans to the pot. Cook and stir until coated. Serve!

Per Serving: Calories 661; Fat 69.63g; Sodium 368mg; Carbs 9.84g; Fiber 3.4g; Sugar 2.15g; Protein 6.47g

Cheese-Bacon Stuffed Peppers

Prep time: 10 minutes | Cook time: 8 minutes | Serves: 4

Ingredients:

8 mini sweet peppers

¼ cup pepper jack cheese, shredded

4 slices sugar-free bacon, cooked and crumbled

4 oz. full-fat cream cheese, softened

Directions:

1. Prepare the peppers by cutting off the tops and halving them lengthwise. Then take out the membrane and the seeds. 2. In a small bowl, mix together the bacon, pepper jack cheese, and cream cheese. 3. Spoon equal-sized portions of the cheese-bacon mixture into each of the pepper halves. 4. Close the lid and move SmartSwitch to AIRFRY/STOVETOP. Select AIR FRY. set temperature to 400°F, and set time to 5 minutes. Press START/STOP to begin preheating. 5. Place the peppers on the crisper tray, then place the crisper tray in the bottom of the pot. Cook for 8 minutes. Serve warm.

Per Serving: Calories 233; Fat 11.12g; Sodium 336mg; Carbs 25.98g; Fiber 3.3g; Sugar 1.69g; Protein 10.86g

Bacon-Wrapped Cheese Jalapeno Popper

Prep time: 15 minutes | Cook time: 13 minutes | Serves: 4

Ingredients:

6 jalapenos

⅓ cup medium cheddar cheese, shredded

¼ tsp. garlic powder

3 oz. full-fat cream cheese

12 slices sugar-free bacon

Directions:

1. To prepare the jalapenos, cut off the tops and slice them lengthwise in half. Be careful while removing the seeds and membranes and consider wearing gloves if needed. 2. Mix cheddar cheese, garlic powder, and cream cheese in a microwave-safe bowl, and heat it in the microwave for 30 seconds. 3. Stir the mixture and spoon equal parts into each jalapeno half. 4. Next, wrap each jalapeno half with a slice of bacon, making sure to cover it completely. 5. Flip the SmartSwitch to AIRFRY/STOVETOP. Select AIR FRY. set temperature to 400°F, and set time to 5 minutes. Press START/STOP to begin preheating. 6. Place the wrapped jalapenos on the crisper tray and repeat with the remaining bacon and jalapeno halves. 7. Place the crisper tray in the bottom of the pot. 8. Cook for 12 minutes, flipping the peppers halfway through the cooking time. Make sure not to let any of the contents spill out of the jalapeno halves when turning them. 9. Serve warm.

Per Serving: Calories 405; Fat 37.11g; Sodium 504mg; Carbs 4.01g; Fiber 0.6g; Sugar 2.78g; Protein 13.91g

Cheesy Bacon Egg Bread

Prep time: 10 minutes | Cook time: 15 minutes | Serves: 2

Ingredients:

4 slices sugar-free bacon, cooked and chopped

2 eggs

¼ cup pickled jalapenos, chopped

¼ cup parmesan cheese, grated

2 cups mozzarella cheese, shredded

Directions:

1. In a bowl, mix together all of the ingredients. 2. Cut out a piece of parchment paper that will fit the base of the crisper tray. 3. With slightly wet hands, roll the mixture into a circle. You may have to form two circles to cook in separate batches. 4. Flip the SmartSwitch to AIRFRY/STOVETOP. Select AIR FRY. set temperature to 320°F, and set time to 5 minutes. Press START/STOP to begin preheating. 5. Place the circle on top of the parchment paper and place on the crisper tray, then place the crisper tray in the bottom of the pot. Cook for 10 minutes. 6. Turn it over and cook for another 5 minutes. 7. The food is ready when it is golden and cooked all the way through. Slice and serve warm.

Per Serving: Calories 433; Fat 20.17g; Sodium 1523mg; Carbs 7.66g; Fiber 2.3g; Sugar 2.8g; Protein 54.23g

Crusted Mozzarella Sticks

Prep time: 500 minutes | Cook time: 10 minutes | Serves: 4

Ingredients:

6 x 1-oz. mozzarella string cheese sticks

1 tsp. dried parsley

½ oz. pork rinds, finely ground

½ cup parmesan cheese, grated

2 eggs

Directions:

1. Cut the mozzarella sticks in half and put them in the freezer for 45 minutes. You may also leave them in the freezer for a longer period and store them in a Ziploc bag. 2. Mix together the dried parsley, pork rinds, and parmesan cheese in a small bowl. In another bowl, beat the eggs using a fork. 3. Flip the SmartSwitch to AIRFRY/STOVETOP. Select AIR FRY. set temperature to 400°F, and set time to 5 minutes. Press START/STOP to begin preheating. 4. Take a mozzarella stick that has been frozen and submerge it into beaten eggs. Dip the mozzarella stick into a mixture of pork rinds, making certain that it is fully coated. 5. Proceed with the rest of the cheese sticks, placing each coated stick on the crisper tray, then place the crisper tray in the bottom of the pot. 6. Cook for 10 minutes, until they are golden brown. 7. Serve hot, with some homemade marinara sauce if desired.

Per Serving: Calories 184; Fat 8.56g; Sodium 596mg; Carbs 3.76g; Fiber 0.8g; Sugar 0.97g; Protein 22.61g

Bacon-Wrapped Brie Cheese

Prep time: 10 minutes | Cook time: 10 minutes | Serves: 1

Ingredients:

4 slices sugar-free bacon

8 oz. brie cheese

Instructions:

1. Flip the SmartSwitch to AIRFRY/STOVETOP. Select AIR FRY. set temperature to 400°F, and set time to 5 minutes. Press START/STOP to begin preheating. 2. Place the bacon slices on a cutting board, arranged in a star shape with two Xs overlaid, and put the round of brie in the middle. 3. Take each bacon slice and wrap it over the brie, securing it with toothpicks. Cut up a piece of parchment paper to fit in your fryer's crisper tray and place it inside, followed by the wrapped brie, setting it in the center of the sheet of parchment, then place the tray in the bottom of the pot. 4. Cook for 7 minutes. Turn the brie over and cook for additional 3 minutes. 5. It is ready once the bacon is crispy and cheese is melted on the inside. 6. Slice up the brie and enjoy hot.

Per Serving: Calories 973; Fat 78.92g; Sodium 2201mg; Carbs 1.8g; Fiber 0g; Sugar 1.02g; Protein 62.66g

Cheese Bacon-Pepperoni Pizza

Prep time: 10 minutes | Cook time: 5 minutes | Serves: 1

Ingredients:

½ cup mozzarella cheese, shredded

7 slices pepperoni

2 slices sugar-free bacon, cooked and crumbled

1 tbsp. parmesan cheese, grated

¼ cup ground sausage, cooked

Directions:

1. Flip the SmartSwitch to AIRFRY/STOVETOP. Select AIR FRY. set temperature to 400°F, and set time to 5 minutes. Press START/STOP to begin preheating. 2. Spread the mozzarella across the bottom of a cake pan that can fit the pot of your Ninja Speedi Rapid Cooker & Air Fryer. 3. Add bacon, sausage, and pepperoni, and sprinkle some parmesan cheese on top. Place the pan on the crisper tray, then place the crisper tray in the bottom of the pot. Cook for 5 minutes. 4. The cheese is ready once brown in color and bubbly. Take care when removing the pan from the fryer and serve.

Per Serving: Calories 300; Fat 16.62g; Sodium 1128mg; Carbs 2.89g; Fiber 1g; Sugar 0.84g; Protein 33.94g

Chapter 7 Dessert Recipes

Eggless Farina Cake

Prep time: 10 minutes | Cook time: 25 minutes | Serves: 6

Ingredients:

Vegetable oil

2 cups hot water

1 cup chopped dried fruit, such as apricots, golden raisins, figs, and/or dates

1 cup farina (or very fine semolina)

1 cup milk

1 cup sugar

¼ cup ghee, butter, or coconut oil, melted

2 tablespoons plain Greek yogurt or sour cream

1 teaspoon ground cardamom

1 teaspoon baking powder

½ teaspoon baking soda

Whipped cream, for serving

Directions:

1. Grease a round baking pan that can fit the pot with vegetable oil. 2. Firstly, mix hot water and dried fruit in a small bowl and keep it aside for 20 minutes to soften the fruit. At the same time, in a large bowl, whisk together farina, milk, yogurt, sugar, ghee, and cardamom. 3. Allow the mixture to stand for 20 minutes so that the farina can absorb the liquid and become soft. 4. Then, drain the dried fruit and add it to the batter, followed by baking powder and baking soda. Mix all the ingredients well. 5. Flip the SmartSwitch to AIRFRY/STOVETOP. Select AIR FRY. set temperature to 325°F, and set time to 5 minutes. Press START/STOP to begin preheating. 6. Pour the batter into the prepared pan. Set the pan on the crisper tray, then place the crisper tray in the bottom of the pot. Cook for 25 minutes, or until a toothpick inserted into the center comes out clean. 7. Allow the cake to cool inside the pan for 10 minutes. Then, remove from the pan and let it cool on the rack for 20 minutes before cutting it into slices. Slice and serve topped with whipped cream.

Per Serving: Calories 232; Fat 11.28g; Sodium 138mg; Carbs 31.65g; Fiber 0.8g; Sugar 26.32g; Protein 2.81g

Cinnamon Almonds

Prep time: 10 minutes | Cook time: 8 minutes | Serves: 4

Ingredients:

1 cup whole almonds

2 tablespoons salted butter, melted

1 tablespoon sugar

½ teaspoon ground cinnamon

Directions:

1. Flip the SmartSwitch to AIRFRY/STOVETOP. Select AIR FRY. set temperature to 300°F, and set time to 5 minutes. Press START/STOP to begin preheating. 2. In a medium bowl, mix together the almonds, sugar, butter, and cinnamon. Toss well to ensure all the almonds are coated with the spiced butter. 3. Place the almonds on the crisper tray in a single layer, then place the tray in the bottom of the pot. Cook for 8 minutes, stirring halfway through the cooking time. 4. Let cool completely before serving.

Per Serving: Calories 44; Fat 3.97g; Sodium 31mg; Carbs 2.32g; Fiber 0.2g; Sugar 1.98g; Protein 0.12g

Chocolate Walnuts Cake

Prep time: 10 minutes | Cook time: 55 minutes | Serves: 4

Ingredients:

Unsalted butter, at room temperature

3 large eggs

1 cup almond flour

⅔ cup sugar

⅓ cup heavy cream

¼ cup coconut oil, melted

¼ cup unsweetened cocoa powder

1 teaspoon baking powder

¼ cup chopped walnuts

Directions:

1. Generously butter a round baking pan that can fit the pot. Place a piece of parchment paper that has been cut to the size of the pan at the bottom of it. 2. Mix the eggs, almond flour, cream, sugar, coconut oil, cocoa powder, and baking powder in a big bowl. Use a hand mixer to beat the mixture until it's thoroughly combined and fluffy. 3. Then add the walnuts and gently stir them in. Flip the SmartSwitch to AIRFRY/STOVETOP. Select BAKE/ROAST, set temperature to 325°F, and set time to 5 minutes. Press START/STOP to begin preheating. 4. Pour the batter into the pan. Cover the pan tightly with aluminum foil. Set the pan on the crisper tray, then place the crisper tray in the bottom of the pot. Bake in the preheated pot for 45 minutes. 5. Remove the foil and cook for 10 to 15 minutes more, until a knife (do not use a toothpick) inserted into the center of the cake comes out clean. 6. Allow the cake to cool inside the pan on a wire rack for a duration of 10 minutes. Remove the cake from the pan and let cool on the rack for 20 minutes before slicing. 7. Slice and serve.

Per Serving: Calories 314; Fat 25.74g; Sodium 20mg; Carbs 21.92g; Fiber 2g; Sugar 16.97g; Protein 4.03g

Zucchini Cakes with Walnuts

Prep time: 10 minutes | Cook time: 15 minutes | Serves: 4

Ingredients:

¼ cup vegetable oil, plus more for greasing

¾ cup all-purpose flour

¾ teaspoon ground cinnamon

¼ teaspoon kosher salt

¼ teaspoon baking soda

¼ teaspoon baking powder

2 large eggs

½ cup sugar

½ cup grated zucchini

¼ cup chopped walnuts

Directions:

1. Generously grease four 4-ounce ramekins or a round baking pan that can fit your pot with vegetable oil. 2. Firstly, sieve together flour, salt, cinnamon, baking soda, and baking powder in a bowl of medium size. 3. Next, beat eggs, sugar, and vegetable oil in another medium bowl. Then, combine the dry ingredients with the wet ones, and mix in the zucchini and nuts until thoroughly blended. Transfer the batter to the prepared ramekins or baking pan. 4. Flip the SmartSwitch to AIRFRY/STOVETOP. Select BAKE/ROAST, set temperature to 325°F, and set time to 5 minutes. Press START/STOP to begin preheating. 5. Place the ramekins or pan on the crisper tray, then place the crisper tray in the bottom of the pot. Cook for 15 minutes, or until a cake tester or toothpick inserted into the center comes out clean. If it doesn't, cook for 3 to 5 minutes more and test again. 6. Let cool in the ramekins or pan on a wire rack for 10 minutes. 7. Carefully remove from the ramekins or pan and let cool completely on the rack before serving.

Per Serving: Calories 313; Fat 19.38g; Sodium 233mg; Carbs 31.95g; Fiber 1.3g; Sugar 12.48g; Protein 4.59g

Lemon Ricotta Poppy Seeds Cake

Prep time: 10 minutes | Cook time: 55 minutes | Serves: 4

Ingredients:

Unsalted butter, at room temperature

1 cup almond flour

½ cup sugar

3 large eggs

¼ cup heavy cream

¼ cup full-fat ricotta cheese

¼ cup coconut oil, melted

2 tablespoons poppy seeds

1 teaspoon baking powder

1 teaspoon pure lemon extract

Grated zest and juice of 1 lemon, plus more zest for garnish

Directions:

1. Generously butter a round baking pan that can fit the pot. Line the bottom of the pan with parchment paper cut to fit. 2. Mix together the almond flour, sugar, eggs, coconut oil, cream, ricotta, baking powder, lemon extract, poppy seeds, lemon zest, and lemon juice in a large bowl. 3. Beat with a hand mixer on medium speed until well blended and fluffy. 4. Flip the SmartSwitch to AIRFRY/STOVETOP. Select BAKE/ROAST, set temperature to 325°F, and set time to 5 minutes. Press START/STOP to begin preheating. 5. Pour the batter into the prepared pan. Cover the pan tightly with aluminum foil. 6. Set the pan on the crisper tray, then place the crisper tray in the bottom of the pot. Bake for 45 minutes. 7. Remove the foil and cook for 10 to 15 minutes more, until a knife (do not use a toothpick) inserted into the center of the cake comes out clean. 8. After baking, allow the cake to cool for 10 minutes in the pan on a wire rack. 9. Then, remove the cake from the pan and let it cool on the rack for an additional 15 minutes before slicing. 10. Sprinkle some extra lemon zest on top, cut into slices, and serve.

Per Serving: Calories 293; Fat 23.84g; Sodium 12mg; Carbs 17.79g; Fiber 1.5g; Sugar 13.38g; Protein 4.9g

Maple Bread Pudding

Prep time: 10 minutes | Cook time: 20 minutes | Serves: 4

Ingredients:

3 slices whole grain bread (preferably a day old), cubed

1 large egg

1 cup whole milk

2 tsp. bourbon

½ tsp. vanilla extract

¼ cup maple syrup, divided

½ tsp. ground cinnamon

2 tsp. sparkling sugar

Directions:

1. Close the lid and move SmartSwitch to AIRFRY/STOVETOP. Select AIR FRY. set temperature to 270°F, and set time to 5 minutes. Press START/STOP to begin preheating. 2. Spray a baking pan that can fit the pot with nonstick cooking spray, then place the bread cubes in the pan. 3. Add the egg, milk, bourbon, 3 tablespoons of maple syrup, vanilla extract, and cinnamon to a medium bowl and mix well. 4. Pour the egg mixture over the bread and press down with a spatula to make sure to coat all the bread, then sprinkle the sparkling sugar on top. 5. Place the pan on the crisper tray, then place the crisper tray in the bottom of the pot. Cook for 20 minutes. 6. Remove the pudding from the fryer and allow to cool in the pan on a wire rack for 10 minutes. Drizzle the remaining 1 tablespoon of maple syrup on top. Slice and serve warm.

Per Serving: Calories 211; Fat 4.32g; Sodium 149mg; Carbs 36.14g; Fiber 2.4g; Sugar 23.03g; Protein 6.62g

Homemade Spice Cookies

Prep time: 10 minutes | Cook time: 12 minutes | Serves: 4

Ingredients:

4 tablespoons (½ stick) unsalted butter, at room temperature

2 tablespoons agave nectar

1 large egg

2 tablespoons water

2½ cups almond flour

½ cup sugar

2 teaspoons ground ginger

1 teaspoon ground cinnamon

½ teaspoon freshly grated nutmeg

1 teaspoon baking soda

¼ teaspoon kosher salt

Directions:

1. Line the bottom of the crisper tray with parchment paper cut to fit. 2. Using a hand mixer, beat the butter, agave, egg, and water in a big bowl until it turns light and fluffy. 3. Then, add the almond flour, sugar, nutmeg, ginger, cinnamon, baking soda, and salt and beat again on low speed until everything is mixed well. 4. Flip the SmartSwitch to AIRFRY/STOVETOP. Select BAKE/ROAST, set temperature to 325°F, and set time to 5 minutes. Press START/STOP to begin preheating. 5. Roll the dough into 2-tablespoon balls and arrange them on the parchment paper on the crisper tray. Then place the tray in the bottom of the pot. Bake for 12 minutes, or until the tops of cookies are lightly browned. 6. Transfer to a wire rack and let the cookies cool completely. Store in an airtight container for up to a week.

Per Serving: Calories 147; Fat 9.36g; Sodium 468mg; Carbs 15.17g; Fiber 0.7g; Sugar 13.37g; Protein 1.44g

Baked Apples

Prep time: 10 minutes | Cook time: 10 minutes | Serves: 4

Ingredients:

4 small apples, cored and cut in half

2 tablespoons salted butter or coconut oil, melted

2 tablespoons sugar

1 teaspoon apple pie spice

Ice cream, heavy cream, or whipped cream, for serving

Directions:

1. Flip the SmartSwitch to AIRFRY/STOVETOP. Select AIR FRY. set temperature to 350°F, and set time to 5 minutes. Press START/STOP to begin preheating. 2. Put the apples into a big bowl, pour the melted butter over them and sprinkle some sugar and apple pie spice on top. 3. Mix everything well using your hands, making sure that the apples are coated with the mixture evenly. 4. Place the apples on the crisper tray, then place the crisper tray in the bottom of the pot. Cook for 10 minutes. Pierce the apples with a fork to ensure they are tender. 5. Serve with ice cream, or top with a splash of heavy cream or a spoonful of whipped cream.

Per Serving: Calories 161; Fat 4.65g; Sodium 58mg; Carbs 31.8g; Fiber 3.6g; Sugar 22.55g; Protein 1.2g

Orange-Anise-Ginger Cookie

Prep time: 10 minutes | Cook time: 15 minutes | Serves: 2-4

Ingredients:

For the Cookie:

Vegetable oil

1 cup plus 2 tablespoons all-purpose flour

1 tablespoon grated orange zest

1 teaspoon ground ginger

1 teaspoon aniseeds, crushed

¼ teaspoon kosher salt

4 tablespoons (½ stick) unsalted butter, at room temperature

½ cup granulated sugar, plus more for sprinkling

3 tablespoons dark molasses

1 large egg

For the Icing:

½ cup confectioners' sugar

2 to 3 teaspoons milk

Directions:

1. For the cookie: Generously grease a round baking pan that can fit the pot with vegetable oil. 2. Combine flour, orange zest, aniseeds, ginger, and salt in a medium bowl by whisking. 3. In another medium bowl, use a hand mixer to beat butter and sugar until well combined, then add molasses and egg and continue beating until the mixture turns light in color. 4. Add the flour mixture and mix on low until it is just combined. Spread the resulting dough evenly into the prepared pan using a rubber spatula, smooth out the top, and sprinkle sugar over it. 5. Flip the SmartSwitch to AIRFRY/STOVETOP. Select BAKE/ROAST, set temperature to 325°F, and set time to 5 minutes. Press START/STOP to begin preheating. 6. Place the pan on the crisper tray, then place the crisper tray in the bottom of the pot. Bake for 15 minutes, or until sides are browned but the center is still quite soft. 7. Let cool in the pan on a wire rack for 15 minutes. Turn the cookie out of the pan onto the rack. 8. For the icing: Whisk together the sugar and 2 teaspoons of milk. Add 1 teaspoon milk if needed for the desired consistency. Spread, or drizzle onto the cookie.

Per Serving: Calories 471; Fat 13.87g; Sodium 217mg; Carbs 81.52g; Fiber 1.3g; Sugar 48.39g; Protein 6.04g

Coconut-Chocolate Cake

Prep time: 10 minutes | Cook time: 55 minutes | Serves: 6

Ingredients:

4 tablespoons (½ stick) unsalted butter, melted, plus room-temperature butter for greasing

½ cup sugar

3 large eggs

½ cup heavy cream

1 teaspoon pure vanilla extract

¼ cup coconut flour

2 tablespoons unsweetened cocoa powder

1 teaspoon baking powder

¼ teaspoon kosher salt

3 tablespoons shredded toasted coconut

Directions:

1. Generously butter a round baking pan that can fit the pot. Line the bottom of the pan with parchment paper cut to fit. 2. In a big bowl, mix together the melted butter and sugar. Add the eggs, cream, and vanilla. Beat with a hand mixer on medium speed until the ingredients are well blended, 2 to 3 minutes. 3. Add the coconut flour, cocoa powder, baking powder, and salt. Beat on low speed until the ingredients are well combined and the batter is relatively smooth. 4. Flip the SmartSwitch to AIRFRY/STOVETOP. Select BAKE/ROAST, set temperature to 325°F, and set time to 5 minutes. Press START/STOP to begin preheating. 5. Pour the batter into the prepared pan. Cover the pan tightly with aluminum foil. 6. Set the pan on the crisper tray, then place the crisper tray in the bottom of the pot. Bake for 45 minutes. 7. Remove the foil and cook for 10 to 15 minutes more, until a knife (do not use a toothpick) inserted into the center of the cake comes out clean. 8. Let the cake cool in the pan on a wire rack for 10 minutes. Remove the cake from the pan and let cool on the rack for 20 minutes before slicing. 9. Slice and serve topped with the toasted coconut.

Per Serving: Calories 151; Fat 11.37g; Sodium 128mg; Carbs 11.08g; Fiber 0.7g; Sugar 9.05g; Protein 2.31g

Easy Cardamom Custard

Prep time: 10 minutes | Cook time: 25 minutes | Serves: 2

Ingredients:

1 cup whole milk

1 large egg

2 tablespoons plus 1 teaspoon sugar

¼ teaspoon vanilla bean paste or pure vanilla extract

¼ teaspoon ground cardamom, plus more for sprinkling

Directions:

1. Close the lid and move SmartSwitch to AIRFRY/STOVETOP. Select BAKE/ROAST, set temperature to 350°F, and set time to 5 minutes. Press START/STOP to begin preheating. 2. In a medium bowl, mix together the milk, egg, vanilla, sugar, and cardamom. 3. Place two 8-ounce ramekins on the crisper tray in the pot. Divide the mixture between the ramekins. Sprinkle lightly with cardamom. 4. Cover each ramekin tightly with aluminum foil. Bake for 25 minutes, or until a toothpick inserted in the center comes out clean. 5. Let the custards cool on a wire rack for 5 to 10 minutes. 6. Serve warm, or refrigerate until cold and serve chilled.

Per Serving: Calories 159; Fat 6.76g; Sodium 72mg; Carbs 18.62g; Fiber 0g; Sugar 18.22g; Protein 5.77g

Yummy Mixed Berry Crumble

Prep time: 10 minutes | Cook time: 15 minutes | Serves: 4

Ingredients:

For the Filling:

2 cups mixed berries, thawed if frozen

2 tablespoons sugar

1 tablespoon cornstarch

1 tablespoon fresh lemon juice

For the Topping:

¼ cup all-purpose flour

¼ cup rolled oats

1 tablespoon sugar

2 tablespoons cold unsalted butter, cut into small cubes

Whipped cream or ice cream (optional)

Directions:

1. To prepare the filling, gently mix berries, sugar, cornstarch, and lemon juice in a round baking pan that can fit the pot. 2. For the topping, combine flour, oats, and sugar in a small bowl, then cut the butter into the mixture until it resembles bread crumbs. Sprinkle the topping over the berries in the pan. 3. Flip the SmartSwitch to AIRFRY/ STOVETOP. Select BAKE/ROAST, set temperature to 400°F, and set time to 5 minutes. Press START/STOP to begin preheating. 4. Place the pan on the crisper tray, then place the crisper tray in the bottom of the pot. Bake for 15 minutes. Let cool for 5 minutes on a wire rack. 5. Serve topped with whipped cream or ice cream, if desired.

Per Serving: Calories 359; Fat 10.65g; Sodium 221mg; Carbs 64.62g; Fiber 3.1g; Sugar 31.76g; Protein 5.09g

Sweet Pineapple Spears

Prep time: 10 minutes | Cook time: 15 minutes | Serves: 4

Ingredients:

½ cup brown sugar

2 teaspoons ground cinnamon

1 small pineapple, peeled, cored, and cut into spears

3 tablespoons unsalted butter, melted

Directions:

1. Combine brown sugar and cinnamon in a small bowl. Then, coat the pineapple spears with melted butter and sprinkle the mixture of cinnamon-sugar on them, gently pressing to make sure it sticks. 2. Flip the SmartSwitch to AIRFRY/STOVETOP. Select AIR FRY. set temperature to 400°F, and set time to 5 minutes. Press START/STOP to begin preheating. 3. Place the spears on the crisper tray in a single layer, then place the tray in the bottom of the pot. (You may have to do this in batches.) Cook for 6-8 minutes per batch. Brush the spears with butter halfway through the cooking time. 4. The pineapple spears are done when they are heated through and the sugar is bubbling. Serve hot.

Per Serving: Calories 273; Fat 6.07g; Sodium 14mg; Carbs 57.71g; Fiber 3.9g; Sugar 48.99g; Protein 1.65g

Chocolate Brownies

Prep time: 10 minutes | Cook time: 15 minutes | Serves: 4

Ingredients:

¼ cup all-purpose flour

¼ tsp. kosher salt

½ tsp. baking powder

3 tsp. unsalted butter, melted

½ cup granulated sugar

1 large egg

3 tsp. unsweetened applesauce

¼ cup miniature semisweet chocolate chips

Coarse sea salt

Directions:

1. Flip the SmartSwitch to AIRFRY/STOVETOP. Select AIR FRY. set temperature to 300°F, and set time to 5 minutes. Press START/STOP to begin preheating. 2. Firstly, mix cocoa powder, all-purpose flour, baking powder, and kosher salt together in a big bowl using a whisk. 3. Then, take another large bowl and combine butter, granulated sugar, egg, and applesauce. After that, use a spatula to combine the cocoa powder mixture and chocolate chips with the butter mixture until they are mixed well. 4. Spray a baking pan that can fit the pot with nonstick cooking spray, then pour the mixture into the pan. 5. Place the pan on the crisper tray, then place the crisper tray in the bottom of the pot. Cook for 15 minutes or until a toothpick comes out clean when inserted in the center. 6. Remove the brownies from the fryer, sprinkle some coarse sea salt on top, and allow to cool in the pan on a wire rack for 20 minutes before cutting and serving.

Per Serving: Calories 174; Fat 7.09g; Sodium 220mg; Carbs 29.37g; Fiber 2.5g; Sugar 18.62g; Protein 3.03g

Homemade Zeppole with Cannoli Dip

Prep time: 10 minutes | Cook time: 10 minutes | Serves: 2

Ingredients:

½ cup all-purpose flour

1¼ tsp. baking powder

2 tsp. granulated sugar

Pinch of kosher salt

½ cup whole milk ricotta cheese

1 large egg, beaten

¼ tsp. vanilla extract

1 tsp. confectioners' sugar

For the Dip:

¼ cup whole milk ricotta cheese

¼ tsp. vanilla extract

2 tsp. nonfat vanilla Greek yogurt

1 tsp. miniature semisweet chocolate chips

Directions:

1. Close the lid and move SmartSwitch to AIRFRY/STOVETOP. Select AIR FRY. set temperature to 390°F, and set time to 5 minutes. Press START/STOP to begin preheating. 2. Combine the all-purpose flour, baking powder, granulated sugar, and kosher salt in a medium bowl and mix well, then add the ricotta cheese, egg, and vanilla extract, stirring until a thick batter forms. 3. Spray the crisper tray with nonstick cooking spray, then place 8 individual tablespoons of batter on the crisper tray, then place the crisper tray in the bottom of the pot. 4. Cook for 5 minutes or until puffed and golden brown. Repeat this process with the remaining batter. 5. As the zeppole are cooking, prepare the dip by mixing ricotta cheese, vanilla extract, vanilla Greek yogurt, and miniature semisweet chocolate chips in a small bowl. Keep it aside. 6. Once the zeppole are cooked, let them cool on a wire rack for 10 minutes and sprinkle confectioners' sugar on them. Serve with the prepared dip.

Per Serving: Calories 742; Fat 40.62g; Sodium 213mg; Carbs 87.79g; Fiber 6g; Sugar 51.49g; Protein 19.19g

Lemony Apple Turnovers

Prep time: 10 minutes | Cook time: 10 minutes | Serves: 4

Ingredients:

1 Granny Smith apple, peeled, quartered, and thinly sliced

½ tsp. pumpkin pie spice

Juice of ½ lemon

1 tsp. granulated sugar

Pinch of kosher salt

6 sheets phyllo dough

Directions:

1. Flip the SmartSwitch to AIRFRY/STOVETOP. Select AIR FRY. set temperature to 330°F, and set time to 5 minutes. Press START/STOP to begin preheating. 2. In a medium bowl, mix together the apple, pumpkin pie spice, granulated sugar, lemon juice, and kosher salt. 3. Cut the phyllo dough sheets into 4 equal pieces and place individual tablespoons of apple filling in the center of each piece, then fold in both sides and roll from front to back. 4. Spray the crisper tray with nonstick cooking spray, then place the turnovers on the tray and place the tray in the bottom of the pot. Cook for 10 minutes or until golden brown. 5. Remove the turnovers from the fryer and allow to cool on a wire rack for 10 minutes before serving.

Per Serving: Calories 114; Fat 1.83g; Sodium 206mg; Carbs 21.87g; Fiber 1.8g; Sugar 4.84g; Protein 2.24g

Blueberry Frosted Pies

Prep time: 10 minutes | Cook time: 24 minutes | Serves: 8

Ingredients:

For the Crust:

1 cup all-purpose flour (plus extra for kneading)

½ tsp. kosher salt

1 tsp. granulated sugar

6 tsp. cold unsalted butter, diced

1–2 tsp. ice water

For the Filling:

½ cup frozen wild blueberries

1 tsp. granulated sugar

2 tsp. water mixed with ¾ tsp. cornstarch

For the Frosting:

¼ cup confectioners' sugar

2 tsp. low-fat milk

Directions:

1. Using a food processor, prepare the crust by blending together all-purpose flour, kosher salt, and granulated sugar. Add the butter and pulse until it breaks down into small pieces. 2. Gradually add ice water, one teaspoon at a time, until the dough comes together in a ball. 3. Shape the dough into a disc on a lightly floured surface and cover it with plastic wrap. Refrigerate for one hour. 4. Flip the SmartSwitch to AIRFRY/STOVETOP. Select BAKE/ROAST, set temperature to 360°F, and set time to 5 minutes. Press START/STOP to begin preheating. 5. While the dough chills, make the filling in a medium microwave-safe bowl by combining the blueberries, granulated sugar, and cornstarch mixture. 6. Cook in the microwave for 2 minutes, stir, and cook for 2 more minutes. 7. Place the dough between 2 pieces of parchment paper and roll into a rectangle. Use a knife to divide the dough into 8 smaller rectangles, then place individual tablespoons of filling on each piece and fold in half over the filling. 8. Use a fork to press and seal the edges and to poke a few holes in the top. 9. Spray the crisper tray with nonstick cooking spray, then place 3–4 pies on the crisper tray, then place the crisper tray in the bottom of the pot. Bake for around 12 minutes. Repeat this process with the remaining pies. 10. As the pies are being cooked, prepare the frosting by mixing confectioners' sugar and milk in a small bowl. 11. Once the pies are done cooking, take them out of the fryer and put them on a wire rack. Then, spread the frosting on top of the pies and let them cool for 10-15 minutes before serving.

Per Serving: Calories 96; Fat 2.12g; Sodium 148mg; Carbs 17.17g; Fiber 0.8g; Sugar 4.39g; Protein 1.77g

Apple Fritters

Prep time: 10 minutes | Cook time: 16 minutes | Serves: 2

Ingredients:

½ cup apple cider

½ cup granulated sugar

2 tsp. coconut oil, melted

1 large egg, beaten

¼ cup buttermilk

1 cup all-purpose flour

¾ cup whole wheat pastry flour

1 tsp. baking powder

¾ tsp. ground cinnamon

⅛ tsp. ground nutmeg

¼ tsp. kosher salt

1 small Gala apple, peeled and finely chopped

1 tsp. confectioners' sugar

Directions:

1. Heat the apple cider in a small saucepan until it boils, then simmer it until it reduces by half. Let it cool after that. 2. In a big bowl, mix together the cider, sugar, egg, coconut oil, and buttermilk using a whisk. Add the whole wheat pastry flour, all-purpose flour, ground cinnamon, ground nutmeg, baking powder, and kosher salt and stir everything together. 3. Add the chopped apple and fold it in. Cover the bowl and put it in the refrigerator for 20 minutes. 4. Close the lid and move SmartSwitch to AIRFRY/STOVETOP. Select BAKE/ROAST, set temperature to 360°F, and set time to 5 minutes. Press START/STOP to begin preheating. 5. Spray a baking pan that can fit the pot with nonstick cooking spray, then place 4 individual tablespoons of dough in the pan. 6. Place on the crisper tray, then place the crisper tray in the bottom of the pot. Bake for 8 minutes or until puffy and golden brown. Repeat this process with the remaining dough. 7. Remove the fritters from the fryer and allow to cool on a wire rack for 10 minutes, then dust with the confectioners' sugar before serving.

Per Serving: Calories 634; Fat 9.05g; Sodium 361mg; Carbs 127.39g; Fiber 9g; Sugar 41.28g; Protein 15.07g

Gluten-Free Chocolate Donut Holes

Prep time: 10 minutes | Cook time: 12 minutes | Serves: 3

Ingredients:

¼ cup warm water

1 tsp. dry active yeast

4 tsp. granulated sugar, divided

2 cups gluten-free baking mix

½ tsp. baking powder

¼ tsp. kosher salt

1 tsp. buttery spread, melted

½ cup whole milk

¼ cup semisweet chocolate chips

Directions:

1. First, mix warm water, dry active yeast, and a teaspoon of granulated sugar in a medium bowl and let it rest for 10 minutes. 2. In a separate large bowl with a dough hook, mix 3 teaspoons of granulated sugar, gluten-free baking mix, baking powder, and kosher salt. 3. Then, pour the yeast mixture, buttery spread, and milk into the dough mixture and stir until the dough comes together and is no longer sticking to the bowl. Let it rest for 30 minutes. 4. Flip the SmartSwitch to AIRFRY/STOVETOP. Select AIR FRY. set temperature to 360°F, and set time to 5 minutes. Press START/STOP to begin preheating. 5. Roll out the dough between 2 pieces of parchment paper until it's ¾-inch thick, then use a small ring mold to cut out 30 small circles. 6. Spray the crisper tray with nonstick cooking spray, then place 8–10 pieces on the crisper tray, then place the crisper tray in the bottom of the pot. 7. Cook for 4 minutes or until puffed and golden brown. Repeat this process with the remaining dough pieces. 8. Remove the donut holes from the fryer and let cool on a wire rack for 10 minutes. 9. While the holes cool, place the semisweet chocolate chips in a medium microwave-safe bowl and cook in the microwave for 1 minute or until melted. 10. Dip each hole in the chocolate, return to the wire rack, and allow to cool for 5 minutes before serving.

Per Serving: Calories 401; Fat 8.05g; Sodium 244mg; Carbs 76.46g; Fiber 9.8g; Sugar 16.8g; Protein 13.2g

Glazed Rainbow Donuts

Prep time: 20 minutes | Cook time: 4 minutes | Serves: 12

Ingredients:

1 tsp. dry active yeast

3 tbsp. granulated sugar (plus 1 tsp.)

2 cups all-purpose flour (plus extra for rolling)

½ tsp. baking powder

¼ tsp. kosher salt

1 tsp. buttery spread, melted

½ cup whole milk (plus 1 tsp. for the glaze)

⅔ cup confectioners' sugar

Rainbow sprinkles (for decorating)

Directions:

1. Mix together water, dry active yeast, and 1 teaspoon of granulated sugar in a small bowl and let it sit for 10 minutes until the yeast becomes active. 2. In the large bowl of a stand mixer fitted with a dough hook, combine the 3 tablespoons of granulated sugar, all-purpose flour, baking powder, and kosher salt. 3. Add the yeast mixture, buttery spread, and ½ cup of milk, and stir until the dough comes away from the sides of the bowl. 4. Cover the dough bowl with a clean dish towel and leave it for 30 minutes until it doubles in size. Roll out the dough on a lightly floured surface and cut out the donuts using two 3½-inch ring molds. Leave the donuts to rest for 20 more minutes. 5. Flip the SmartSwitch to AIRFRY/STOVETOP. Select AIR FRY. set temperature to 360°F, and set time to 5 minutes. Press START/STOP to begin preheating. 6. Spray the crisper tray with nonstick cooking spray, then place 3 donuts on the tray and place tray in the bottom of the pot. Cook for 4 minutes. Repeat this process with the remaining donuts. 7. While the donuts cook, make the glaze in a small bowl by whisking together the confectioners' sugar and 1 tablespoon of milk until smooth. 8. Remove the donuts from the fryer and place on a wire rack to cool for 5 minutes, then dip in the glaze and top with the sprinkles. Set aside for 20 minutes before serving.

Per Serving: Calories 117; Fat 0.63g; Sodium 61mg; Carbs 25.05g; Fiber 0.7g; Sugar 8.81g; Protein 2.66g

Conclusion

Are you seeking to begin your weight loss journey and embrace a healthier way of life? The Ninja Speedi is the perfect choice for you! This versatile 12-in-1 kitchen appliance can air fry, crisp, roast, bake, broil, reheat, and dehydrate meats and vegetables, making it the perfect choice for whipping up healthier desserts and snacks. With its advanced technology, this all-in-one appliance removes excess fats from your food while still achieving the desired level of crispiness. Plus, its high-capacity pot and dishwasher-safe accessories make it easy to cook for the whole family. And if you need some inspiration, the included cookbook offers plenty of delicious and nutritious meal ideas. Start your journey to a healthier lifestyle today with the Ninja Speedi!

Appendix 1 Measurement Conversion Chart

VOLUME EQUIVALENTS (LIQUID)

US STANDARD	US STANDARD (OUNCES)	METRIC (APPROXIMATE)
2 tablespoons	1 fl.oz	30 mL
¼ cup	2 fl.oz	60 mL
½ cup	4 fl.oz	120 mL
1 cup	8 fl.oz	240 mL
1½ cup	12 fl.oz	355 mL
2 cups or 1 pint	16 fl.oz	475 mL
4 cups or 1 quart	32 fl.oz	1 L
1 gallon	128 fl.oz	4 L

VOLUME EQUIVALENTS (DRY)

US STANDARD	METRIC (APPROXIMATE)
⅛ teaspoon	0.5 mL
¼ teaspoon	1 mL
½ teaspoon	2 mL
¾ teaspoon	4 mL
1 teaspoon	5 mL
1 tablespoon	15 mL
¼ cup	59 mL
½ cup	118 mL
¾ cup	177 mL
1 cup	235 mL
2 cups	475 mL
3 cups	700 mL
4 cups	1 L

TEMPERATURES EQUIVALENTS

FAHRENHEIT(F)	CELSIUS（C）(APPROXIMATE)
225 ℉	107 ℃
250 ℉	120 ℃
275 ℉	135 ℃
300 ℉	150 ℃
325 ℉	160 ℃
350 ℉	180 ℃
375 ℉	190 ℃
400 ℉	205 ℃
425 ℉	220 ℃
450 ℉	235 ℃
475 ℉	245 ℃
500 ℉	260 ℃

WEIGHT EQUIVALENTS

US STANDARD	METRIC (APPROXINATE)
1 ounce	28 g
2 ounces	57 g
5 ounces	142 g
10 ounces	284 g
15 ounces	425 g
16 ounces (1 pound)	455 g
1.5 pounds	680 g
2 pounds	907 g

Appendix 2 Recipes Index

Made in United States
Troutdale, OR
11/25/2023

14892679R00067